High Street looking south in 1809, with the second Town Hall on the right.

CROYDON
A Pictorial History

Oak Alley in 1893. The jettied, timber-framed building on the right had once been a public house – the *Blackamoor's Head*, and later, the *Green Man*.

CROYDON
A Pictorial History

John B. Gent

Phillimore

1991

Published by
PHILLIMORE & CO. LTD.,
Shopwyke Hall, Chichester, Sussex

© John B. Gent

ISBN 0 85033 800 X

Printed and bound in Great Britain by
BIDDLES LTD.,
Guildford, Surrey

To the late Kenneth Malcolm King ('Smiler'), schoolmaster at Selhurst Grammar School, and the late Kenneth Arthur Ryde, Reference Librarian at Croydon, whose enthusiasm for Croydon's history stimulated mine.

List of Illustrations

Frontispiece: Oak Alley, 1893

Select Bibliography

Anderson, J. Corbet, *A Chronicle of Croydon* (1882)

Broadbent, U. and Latham, R. (ed.), *Coulsdon, Downland Village* (1976)

Garrow, The Rev. D. W., *The History and Antiquities of Croydon* (1818)

Gent, J. B. (ed.), *Croydon, The Story of a Hundred Years*, 6th edn. (1988)

Gent, J. B. (ed.), *Croydon Between the Wars* (1987)

Gent, J. B. (ed.), *Croydon Old and New*, 3rd edn. (1980)

Gent, J. B. (ed.), *Edwardian Croydon Illustrated*, 2nd edn. (1990)

Gent, J. B. (ed.), *Victorian Croydon Illustrated*, 2nd edn. (1990)

McInnes, P., Sparkes, B. and Broderick, P., *One Hundred Years of Croydon At Work* (1991)

Paget, Clarence G., *By-Ways in the History of Croydon* (1929)

Paget, Clarence G., *Croydon Homes of the Past* (1937)

Pelton, J. O., *Relics of Old Croydon* (1891)

Steinman, G. S., *A History of Croydon* (1834)

Warwick, Alan R., *The Phoenix Suburb* (1972)

Winterman, Mrs. M. A., *Croydon's Parks, An Illustrated History* (1988)

Acknowledgements

I am very grateful for the assistance that I have received in preparing this book. In particular I must thank Dr. Ron Cox for reading the manuscript, providing additional information and making some extremely constructive suggestions and comments; Mike Hutchins for reading and checking the manuscript; Steve Roud and the staff at Croydon Local Studies Library for their unfailing patience, help, and permission to use illustrations from the local collection; Ken Woodhams for preparing and modifying several maps and diagrams; Muriel Shaw for her notes on local archaeology; and Bernard Milland for help with typing. Dave Smith (*Memories of Hendon*) produced excellent copies from some faded original photographs, and Ken Carr, John Holder, Geoff Rollason, Tom Samson and Messrs. Chorley and Handford Ltd., kindly provided photographs and gave permission for their reproduction. Tim Harding, Rob Marsden, Tony Moss, Roger Packham, Sally Peake, Freddie Percy, Lilian Thornhill and Phillip Truett have also been very helpful.

The illustrations are from the following sources: Croydon Local Studies Library: Inside front cover, frontispiece, 4-7, 9-13, 16-29, 32-34, 41, 42, 54, 55, 57, 60, 63, 80-82, 84, 91, 113, 114, 115, 118, 131, 134, 137, 138, 140, 142, 150, 153-58, 160, 162, 163, 167, 170, 174, 175, Inside back cover; Croydon Natural History and Scientific Society: 3; Messrs. Chorley and Handford Ltd: 178; London Borough of Croydon, Department of Development: 1; The John Gent Collection: 8, 14, 15, 30, 31, 35-40, 43-53, 56, 58, 59, 61, 62, 64-79, 83, 85-90, 92-96, 98-100, 102-12, 116, 117, 119-130, 132, 133, 135, 136, 139, 141, 143, 146-9, 151, 152, 159, 161, 164-6, 168, 169, 171-3, 176, 177, 179; John Holder: 101; Pamlin Prints: 97; Geoff Rollason: 145; and Ken Woodhams: 2.

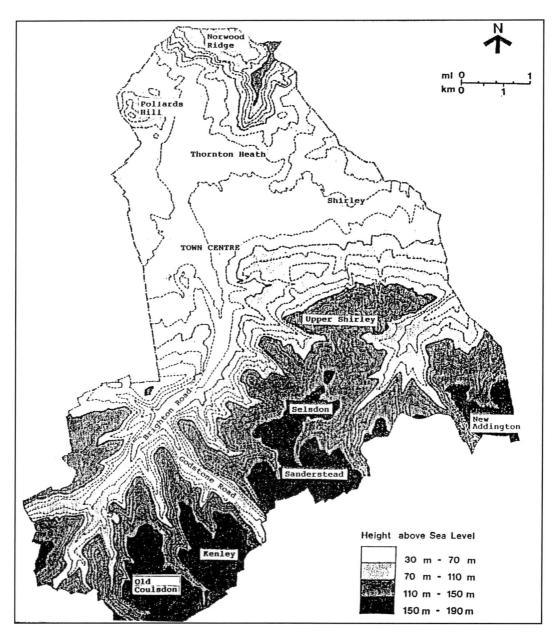

1. This plan of the topography of the borough is based on one prepared by the London Borough of Croydon's Department of Planning and Transportation. Croydon is situated on the southern border of the London Basin at the foot of the long slope of the North Downs, here at their widest and highest reaching 882 ft. (240m.) above sea level at Botley Hill. Lower lying Tertiary formations overlie the downland chalk and are exposed in a northward progression across the borough, comprising, in ascending order, sands of the Thanet Beds, loams and clays of the Woolwich and Reading Beds and heavier clays of the London Clay. Pebble and sand of the Blackheath Beds largely replace the Woolwich and Reading Beds on the eastern side of the town, and due to their greater resistance to erosion form higher ground (and extend further up the downland slope) as clearly seen at Addington Hills and Croham Hurst. High on the Downs remnants of Tertiary beds provide a thin covering of Clay-with-Flints. The Norwood ridge, a long narrow hill in London Clay which escaped erosion, is a dominant feature of northern Croydon, reaching 376 ft. (104m.) above sea level. The lesser Pollards Hill to the west is also fairly prominent.

   Early settlement developed on the River Wandle where its valley emerged from the downland. Meltwater drainage in the Ice Age carved an intricate system of deep narrow valleys in the downland slope. As the climate ameliorated they became dry and the Wandle was much reduced in length. The flint debris washed out of the downland valley system in the Ice Age remains. The modern centre of the town stands on the gravels of the Fairfield Terrace, with Old Town on the lower Mitcham Terrace.

   Diversity of soils gives the borough a variety of landscape and vegetation – heath and birch/pine woodland on the Tertiary sands, mixed oak woodland on the clays, with beechwood and grassland on the chalk.

Introduction

'In the midst of a country rich in the beauties of cultivated nature stands the ancient town of Croydon'. Within a lifetime this quotation from the *Illustrated Guide to the South Eastern Railway* for 1858 would have seemed a little strange. From the mid-19th century Croydon's population was increasing more rapidly than anywhere else in the South East outside London and much of the surrounding countryside was rapidly being covered by 'desirable residences', churches, schools and factories.

But Croydon is an ancient town and despite 150 years of continuing urban growth it still retains many attractive reminders of 'the beauties of cultivated nature'. Domesday Book details two manors, Croydon and Waddon, but there were certainly others in later years and its boundaries remained virtually unchanged until well into the 20th century. In 1883 Croydon achieved borough status, earlier attempts in 1691 and 1707 having been unsuccessful, and six years later became a county borough, having the same administrative status as a county. In 1928 it absorbed the ancient parish of Addington, also mentioned in Domesday Book. Meanwhile the Urban District of Coulsdon and Purley had been formed in 1915 to administer the ancient parishes of Coulsdon and Sanderstead, both also recorded in Domesday Book. In 1965 this was merged with Croydon which then became, in terms of population, the largest of the new London Boroughs and the eighth largest town in the country. Croydon's even greater development has been hampered only by its location on the extreme eastern edge of the County of Surrey by the restrictive practices of medieval archbishops who had a residence there and were lords of the manor, and in the 20th century by the presence of London on its doorstep. It must be said, however, that London has had a significant influence on the town in terms of trade, and in providing much of its growing population. Croydon now provides employment for some 150,000 people, many of whom commute to the town daily – particularly from Kent, Surrey and Sussex – mostly by car or by using the railways that make the town's East station one of the busiest in the country. Although now part of the urban mass of Greater London, Croydon retains an independence of spirit and most of the facilities of a large provincial city. It also suffers from many of the problems of such a city, in particular traffic congestion.

The towering office blocks in the town centre are a landmark for miles around and the town has been likened to a 'Mini Manhattan'. Some like it, some do not, but there can be no doubting the bustling vitality of the place and the benefits of local employment and facilities that have come with new developments since the 1960s. However, Croydon is not just the town centre. The local districts each have their own individuality and Croydon is fortunate that only a very short distance from its heart there are hundreds of acres of virtually unspoilt Surrey countryside in considerable variety including ancient woodland, farmland, rolling downland and attractive parkland. With a few ancient churches and other venerable buildings set amidst its miles of suburban streets as a reminder of its antiquity, it is a town of great variety and contrasts – some good and some not so good. But for centuries it was just a small market town, separated from London by large commons, farms, fields and the Great North Wood which was the haunt of gypsies and highwaymen. The little communities of Addington, Coulsdon and Sanderstead were even more remote from the outside world, remaining isolated well into the 20th century.

Numerous books have been written about various aspects of Croydon's history. This once provides a brief summary of its story to the present day, concentrating on the town and ancient parish, but not ignoring the more recent additions to its administrative area. Most of the illustrations have not been published before but a few that may be familiar have been included where they illustrate a point particularly well. More than half are from the author's own collection, including some 80 picture postcards. Others are mainly from the fine collection of Croydon Local Studies Library. The Librarian there is keen to add to the collection and would be interested to hear from readers who have local photographic – or indeed any other – record material that they would be prepared to donate or loan for copying purposes.

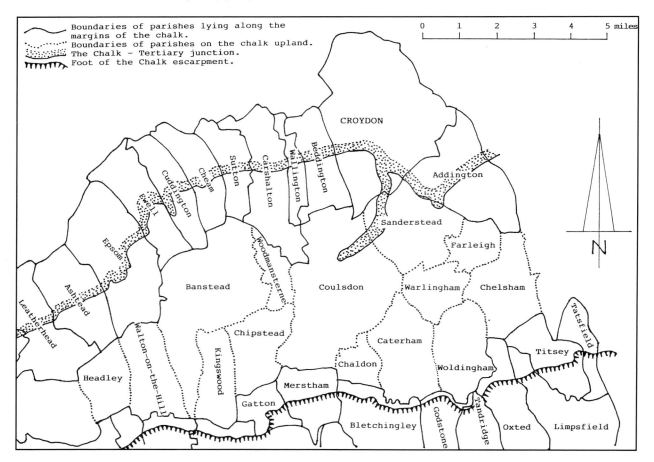

2. The boundaries of Saxon estates usually remained as parish boundaries until the Victorian period and have in many cases survived, at least in part, recent local government upheavals. In common with all the 20 Surrey parishes along the 24-mile northern edge of the dip slope of the North Downs between the Kent boundary and Guildford, Croydon was elongated from north to south, and relatively narrow from east to west. It was however at least twice the size of any of the others, which may reflect its importance as a possession of the archbishops. Each parish included land suitable for pasture and woodland on the clay to the north, and chalk downland suitable for grazing sheep to the south and, in between, more fertile land on a mix of soils suitable for arable purposes. The main settlement of the estate/parish was inevitably on the spring line, where water came to the surface at the junction of the chalk and clay lands. This plan illustrates the point by showing the parishes between Croydon and Leatherhead, and those on the Downs to the south.

Beginnings to 1851

The early history of Croydon is very obscure. The name is of Saxon origin and may mean the 'valley where wild saffron grows'. Some other local names date from the same period and a number remind us of the densely wooded nature of the area. The original settlement grew up just to the north of an important gap and series of valleys through the North Downs and on the headwaters of the River Wandle.

The area lacks conspicuous field monuments, but traces of man's activities dating from eight to ten thousand years ago can be found in the Wandle valley and on the surrounding downlands. There are one or two flint hand-axes older than this, but there are greater numbers of worked flints left behind by the nomadic hunters and gatherers of the Middle Stone age and farmers of later prehistoric times. From about 1000 B.C. finds of flints, pottery, animal bones and metalwork mark small scattered settlements at Park Hill; and in the Wandle valley at Beddington and Waddon. Hoards of bronze implements found at Shirley, Addington, Purley, Coulsdon, Beddington and Carshalton indicate trading by itinerant smiths probably based on the important Bronze Age site at Queen Mary's Hospital at Carshalton.

Occupation continued on the sites at Park Hill, Beddington and Waddon up to the Roman period, and at Atwood School, Sanderstead, there was a larger settlement dating from the first century B.C. to the first century A.D. A Roman period settlement is indicated in the later town centre by a considerable scatter of coins and pottery, and a small amount of building material and metalwork. A small group of Roman type burials and the possibility of other undated skeletons being of the same period adds to this evidence. There were also four hoards of Roman coins dated between the second and fourth centuries A.D.

3. This Roman hunt cup from the third century was found at Croydon in 1880.

Since a minor Roman road (London to Portslade) went through Croydon, probably along the line of the present High Street, it is likely that the settlement was a posting station, being about ten miles from London. To the east, another road (London to Lewes) forms part of the boundary between Croydon/Surrey and Kent, and a considerable amount of Roman material has been found nearby in the Addington and West Wickham areas. The nearest known Roman building to Croydon is the villa at Beddington, which apparently belonged to a native Briton who adopted a Roman lifestyle.

The largest quantity of coins, pottery amd metalwork yet found in Croydon came from Whitgift Street. Here also, a small amount of early Saxon pottery provided a link with the fifth and sixth century A.D. cemetery in nearby Edridge Road, on the slope to the east. This, with the nearby cemeteries of similar date at Beddington and Mitcham, would have belonged to some of the earliest Saxon immigrants to this country.

It is assumed that the Croydon Saxon settlement grew up in the Old Town area near the parish church, where there is evidence of a Saxon church. Later Saxon activity, marked by domestic debris and coins, hints at the probability of a Saxon manor house, predecessor of the Old Palace, and, from the presence of Roman building material, an even earlier building. The plentiful water supply here would have been attractive for settlement but brought other problems. As early as the 13th century it was referred to as 'Le Eldetoun' indicating that the main settlement had already moved up the slope to the aptly named High Street area to avoid dampness and flooding.

Saxon occupation of the Downs at Sanderstead, Riddlesdown, Purley and Coulsdon is indicated by sixth- and seventh- century burial graves, while on Farthing Down there is a more impressive cemetery, where some 40 burials were discovered under and between barrows. Predating the cemetery are traces of a field system used in Romano-British times.

The only indication of Viking activity in the area comes from a hoard of silver pennies, some foreign coins and scraps of metal buried about A.D. 875 near Thornton Heath, then part of the Great North Wood.

Evidence indicates that Croydon belonged to the archbishops of Canterbury as early as the seventh or eighth century. A synod was held in Croydon in 809 and this suggests that it could have been a centre of some religious importance, the church being, perhaps, a minster church from which priests were sent out to more isolated and heathen parts of the area. Domesday Book records a church and a mill, and, by the Middle Ages, Croydon church was the centre of a rural deanery. The structure itself was one of the largest in the county. The adjacent manor house, now the Old Palace, contains fragments of Norman work. Croydon House, as it was called, grew in size and importance as the manor of Lambeth became the London residence of the archbishops. Journeys between London and Canterbury could not be undertaken quickly by the archbishop and his large retinue, and suitable resting places were needed en route. Croydon was only one of a chain of manor houses between 10 and 15 miles apart but, being near London, it was also most suitable as a rural retreat. Set amidst clear trout streams and wooded lands with a deer park at nearby Park Hill, it offered the seclusion necessary. The settlement of Croydon was not large but Archbishop Kilwardby in 1273 obtained a grant for a market to be held every Wednesday, and in 1276 for a nine-day fair each May. This does suggest that, although small, the town was already of some importance as a trading centre.

The archbishops, and the presence of their palace, had a considerable influence. Periodically, Croydon House became the focal point of great activity. Monarchs who stayed there before 1400 include the first three Edwards. From around 1400 the manor

4. John Whitgift became Bishop of Worcester in 1577 and Archbishop of Canterbury in 1583. He developed a great affection for Croydon and frequently stayed at the palace, entertaining Queen Elizabeth I there on numerous occasions. In 1595 he obtained Letters Patent from the Queen authorising him to found a hospital or almshouse at Croydon to be called the Hospital of the Holy Trinity and in 1596 he included a school in the endowment. Various farms and land in the parish were purchased and conveyed to the hospital. Whitgift died in 1604 and was buried in Croydon parish church, where there is a fine memorial to him.

5. William Laud was Bishop of Bath and Wells in 1626, became Bishop of London in 1629 and Archbishop of Canterbury in 1633. He spent a great deal of time at Croydon. One of his first acts as archbishop was to replace the old altar in the chapel at Croydon Palace, which he moved to the east end and railed off with closely spaced balusters to keep out stray dogs. In 1640 he was declared a traitor by the House of Commons, was arrested and was beheaded at Tower Hill in 1645.

increased in size and importance. Later monarchs to stay included Henry IV, Henry VI, Henry VII, Mary and Elizabeth I. In August and September 1556, 23 meetings of the Privy Council took place there. The presence of members of the Royal retinue and other officials all requiring accommodation and refreshment on the occasion of these, and numerous other visits by important people, placed severe demands on the town, but brought opportunities for trade.

By 1640 Croydon was one of the principal towns in the county although of lesser importance than Guildford, Kingston or Farnham. However, it was the most important town in East Surrey and during the Civil War was the administrative centre for the County Committee when it was not meeting at Kingston. In 1647 General Fairfax stayed in the town for several days and is described as having brought half his army there.

During the 18th century the presence of troops in the area from time to time required billeting and whilst this brought trade, it also worried the townspeople as it caused a shortage of accommodation at market and fair times. Several petitions were submitted to the government and eventually in 1794 barracks were established at Mitcham Road, although this seems merely to have alleviated the problem and not solved it.

Croydon's main claim to fame in the Middle Ages was as a source of London's fuel. Charcoal was used as the principal fuel until coal was brought by sea; in other parts of the south, notably the Weald, it was extensively used for industrial purposes, particularly iron making. The vast woods around the town and especially to the north, provided the charcoal burners, known as colliers, with a plentiful supply of timber. The smoke from their fires upset at least one of the archbishops and several 16th- and 17th-century poems and plays refer to the Croydon Colliers, who seem to have been a topic for satire and merriment. Greene, in his *Quip for an upstart Courtier*, of 1592, wrote: 'Marry, quoth he that lookt like Lucifer, though I am black, I am not the divell, but indeed a Collyer of Croydon'. A poem by Patrick Hannay, published in 1662, includes the following, not very complimentary description:

> In midst of these stands Croydon cloath'd in black,
> In a low bottome sinke of all these hills;
> And is receipt of all the durtie wracke,
> Which from their tops still in abundance trils;
> The unpav'd lanes with muddie mire it fills,
> If one shower fall, or if that blessing stay,
> You may well smell, but neuer see your way.

The industry declined generally and not just in Croydon towards the end of the 18th century when there was concern over depletion of woodland and when new methods of iron smelting came into use. It seems to have died out completely in the Croydon area by the end of the century but the name of Colliers Water Lane in Thornton Heath is a permanent reminder of a once important local industry.

To return to the palace, Hutton was the last archbishop to stay there, in 1757. It was at the time described as being 'in a low and unwholesome situation, incommodious and unfit to be the habitation of an Archbishop of Canterbury', so succeeding archbishops did not use it and in 1780 it was sold to become a factory, and later a school. The long association of the archbishops with the area was resumed, however, when Addington Palace was purchased and used as a rural retreat between 1808 and 1896. Six of the archbishops were buried in Croydon parish church while five were buried at Addington. Croydon Deanery remained in the Diocese of Canterbury – an island some 30 miles away from the nearest other place in the diocese – until 1985, when it was incorporated in the Diocese of Southwark.

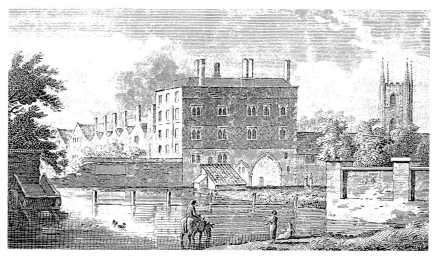

6. Croydon manor was held by the archbishops of Canterbury from before Domesday. Their manor house, later known as Croydon Palace, was adjacent to the old parish church of St John the Baptist. This view shows part of the palace from the north-east, looking across the Great Pond in 1808. In 1758 the archbishops had ceased to use the building and it was sold in 1780, becoming a factory, and later a school. Parts of the palace survive, including the great hall dating from 1443-52 with a magnificent hammer-beam roof of Spanish chestnut, the chapel of the same century, the long gallery and the guard room.

7. Metal trade tokens were issued at some 55 different places in Surrey. Used instead of small-value coins, their issue commenced about 1648 but was stopped some 30 years later by Royal proclamation. Tokens were again issued in considerable quantities in the late 18th and 19th centuries. Several examples such as this one, dated 1797, were issued in Croydon.

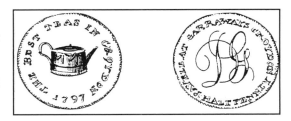

Croydon's market was especially noted for grain and in the 17th century was a major supplier of corn for London. Defoe, writing in the 1720s, described the town as '... a great corn market but chiefly for oats and oatmeal, all for London still ...'. William Page, in his 'Recollections' of Croydon in the 1820s described the market as being in three parts; for provisions, livestock and corn. The provision market was housed in the Butter Market House in High Street, the livestock market was held in Butcher Row opposite the *Three Tuns* inn and the corn market was held in the Town Hall, then in the High Street.

In the early 19th century a cherry fair was held in July and a walnut fair in October. The latter was recorded as early as 1644 and its importance seems to have been more than local as one writer stated that 'it was an article of popular faith that walnuts came in at Croydon Fair'.

To cater for all these activities inns played an important role. The best known names included the *Blue Anchor*, the *Crown*, the *Green Dragon*, the *George*, the *Greyhound*, the *King's Arms*, the *Three Tuns* and the *White Lion* but there were other quite important establishments and numerous ale houses. The *Greyhound*, although it may not have been a principal coaching inn, was recorded as early as 1493 and played an important role in the town's social and administrative life in the absence of a purpose-built town hall before 1809.

8. The location of the fair for which Archbishop Kilwardby obtained a charter in 1276 is not recorded – in the early days fairs were often held in the streets – but the Fair Field was named in a 1493 survey. This print, published by William Annan of the High Street, depicts the fair on 2 October 1833. Appropriately the town's main entertainment centre, Fairfield Halls, now stands on part of the site.

9. This Market House for the sale of butter and poultry, for example, was built at the expense of Francis Tyrrell, grocer and citizen of London, who was a native of Croydon. It is thought to have been Croydon's first Town Hall. Market houses in many parts of the country were used for parochial business and this often led to them being called town halls. This one stood near the corner of Butcher Row (now Surrey Street) and High Street, and was replaced by a second town hall in 1809.

The Winter Quarter Sessions of the county were held in the town and the Assizes alternated between there and Guildford until 1887. Accommodation for judges and lawyers was required and the inns provided some of this. A military survey of 1686 recorded 117 guest beds and stabling for 359 horses in the town. By a later survey in 1756 there were 781 guest beds and 1,220 stablings, substantially more than anywhere else in the county. The turnpike trusts had brought modest improvement to some roads by then and the position of the town on a busy coaching route no doubt at least partly accounts for the increase.

The end of the 18th century brought two events which were to have a profound effect on Croydon's later development. The first was the enclosure of the common lands; and the second the development of proposals for a canal and a railway to the town.

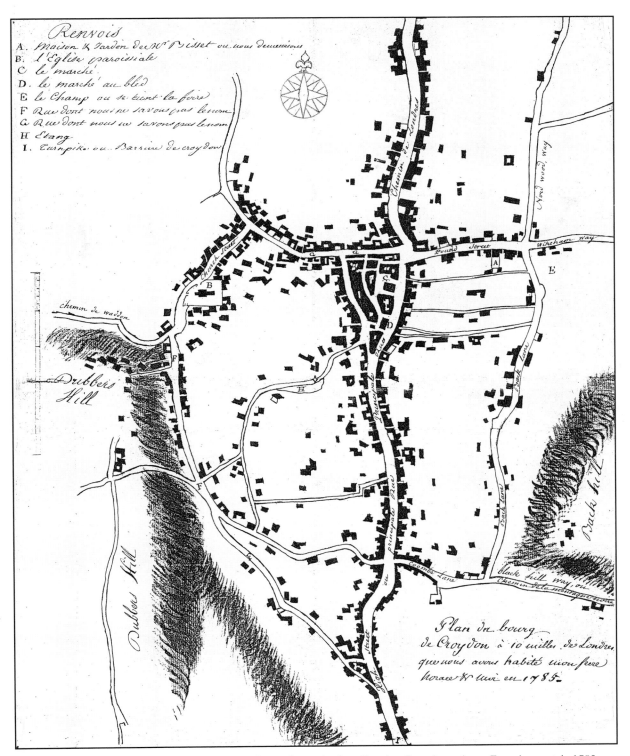

10. This is the earliest known plan of the town. It was drawn by Jean Baptiste Say, the eminent French *savant*, in 1785. He and his brother stayed for some time with Alexander Bisset who kept an academy for gentlemen in Pound Steet. The key, translated from the French, is: A – House and garden of Mr. Bissett, B – Parish Church, C – Market, D – Corn Market, E – Field where the Fair is held, F and G – Roads of which we do not know the name, H – Pond, I – Turnpike Gate. Coombe Road is described as Black Hill Way or the Way to the Black Mountain. This was probably a misunderstanding of the name Back or Park Hill.

11.   Much of the parish remained completely rural until the mid-19th century. The precise location of this 1823 scene at Norwood is not known but it is thought to show Fox's Farm and the view down Fox Hill. The panorama from the Norwood ridge was, and is, very extensive. The Great North Wood covered a large area extending from Forest Hill and Dulwich to Norbury and Selhurst.

12.   This 1825 view shows the toll-gate of the Surrey and Sussex Turnpike Trust in South End, looking north from outside the *Swan & Sugar Loaf*. Behind the toll-house (right) is the cupola on the stables of Blunt House, a fine mansion which, until 1889, stood between the sites of the present Aberdeen and Ledbury Roads. Blunt House was latterly the residence of Sir George Gilbert Scott, the celebrated architect, and his son, John Oldrid Scott. The *Blue Anchor* is immediately beyond the gate, with Southbridge Lane to the left. On the extreme left is the Bourne stream, which is a source of the River Wandle. Selsdon Road is to the right.

13.   The horses of a stagecoach are being changed outside the *Green Dragon*, one of the town's principal coaching inns, as a pack-horse is led along the High Street. In 1830, the date of this drawing, the timbered building behind the coach, at the junction of Butcher Row and High Street, was occupied by James Battersbee, a grocer, and the shops on the right by Thomas Corker, a currier and leather cutter, and William Bullock, a boot and shoe maker. The 1809 Town Hall with its cupola is opposite the *Ship Inn*, the T-shaped sign of which is clearly visible.

The enclosure movement had started with an Act of 1756 designed to preserve forests and the growth of timber for naval requirements. A further Act of 1773 was intended to improve cultivation of common arable fields, wastes and commons and to secure a better food supply for the general population. The good of the community at large was intended to be paramount but specific private acts often included clauses that did not work for the general good and extinguished common rights enjoyed for centuries. An application by various local gentlemen for the enclosure of Croydon's common lands resulted in an Act being passed in 1797. Some 2,950 acres of open and common fields, commons, marshes, heath, waste and commonable woods, were involved. About 230 acres were set aside for the inhabitants. These were to be administered by trustees, but as the plots were in 28 fragmented lots around the parish they proved of little benefit and the trustees shortly obtained an Act empowering them to sell the land and use the proceeds for the building of a new town hall and butter market, and the creation of an enlarged burial ground at the parish church.

There was a right to object to the details of enclosures but the Croydon Act specifically prescribed that 'claimants must send in their claims in Writing under their Hands or the Hands of their Agents, distinguishing in such Claims the Tenure of their Estates in respect whereof such Claims are made, and stating therein such further Particulars as shall be necessary to describe such Claims with Precision.' As J. L. and Barbara Hammond commented in *The Village Labourer*:

> the cottager, unable to read or write ... knowing only that as long as he can remember he has always kept a cow, driven his geese across the waste, pulled his fuel out of the neighbouring brushwood and cut turf from the common, and that his father did all these things before him, was not likely to be able to make a legal case to support his rights.

Nearly a third of the parish of Croydon up to that time had been available for the general use of the inhabitants. As a result of enclosure the land later became available for the benefit of the new owners, and for later development to their great profit as the town expanded.

As regards the canal and the railway, by 1793 England was at war with France. Bulky goods had to go by sea between London and the south coast because of the inadequate roads. A safe inland route was required and by the end of the century interested parties were producing ideas for canals or railways south of London. Croydon was the first objective but the important naval port of Portsmouth was seen as the ultimate goal.

The River Wandle was at that time very heavily industrialised and in 1799 a group of local industrialists proposed a canal up the valley. William Jessop, their engineer, thought that the water supply for a canal would affect the mills and proposed instead an iron railway. There had for several centuries been horse-drawn railways in the collieries and quarries of the North and Midlands, but they were private lines and nearly all used wooden rails.

Eventually in 1801, the Surrey Iron Railway Act was passed and construction started on the first public railway in the world. The line commenced at Wandsworth and ran through Mitcham to Croydon, with a branch from Mitcham to Hackbridge. The Surrey Iron Railway (S.I.R.) opened in 1803 and an extension, the Croydon, Merstham & Godstone Railway (C.M.G.R.) in 1805. The latter actually only reached Merstham, where it served the stone quarries and firestone mines. The railways were horse-drawn and were used only for freight.

Meanwhile, there had been several schemes for a canal from the Thames at Deptford to Croydon, and several weeks after Parliament authorised the S.I.R. it also authorised the Croydon Canal. This opened in 1809, passing through delightful countryside almost completely devoid of population. It needed 26 locks to surmount the rise of 150 ft. (45m.) between New Cross and Forest Hill, with two more at Selhurst. A short length of iron railway linked the canal wharf at Croydon with the main S.I.R. and C.M.G.R. line at Pitlake near the parish church. The alignment is now followed by Tamworth Road.

Traffic on both the canal and the railways consisted mainly of coal, timber, stone, groceries, corn, fuller's earth and lime. The canal was also extensively used for pleasure purposes – angling, boating and, in winter, skating.

Thus by 1809 Croydon had a railway and a canal, but it is very doubtful whether the trade of the area justified the two competing forms of transport and neither seems to have prospered. The proprietors' dreams of reaching Portsmouth were never achieved. The threat from France had receded and steam railways were in their infancy. By the 1830s the canal was giving problems – the banks at Forest Hill collapsed several times and the bed leaked in the Penge Common area – and it proved difficult to maintain water levels. In 1834 the London & Croydon Railway Company was formed and decided to purchase and drain the canal, using it partly as the alignment for a railway worked by steam locomotives.

14.   The precise location of this 1820 drawing by the prolific artist, James Bourne, is not recorded. It shows a swing- or draw-bridge and it is thought there were some 30 similar bridges over the canal, mainly for farm tracks. Several of them were near the Croydon end of the canal.

It was at that time thought necessary and desirable to have only one railway route south from London, so the London & Brighton and South Eastern Railway companies had to use the London & Croydon route, which itself started out over the London & Greenwich Railway's line between London Bridge and Corbett's Lane, Bermondsey. The Brighton and South Eastern companies' tracks left the Croydon's route at Selhurst and then shared the line to Redhill whence the Brighton continued south to the coast and the South Eastern turned east to Tonbridge, Ashford and Dover.

The canal closed in 1836. The London & Croydon opened in 1839 followed by the London & Brighton in 1841 and the South Eastern in 1842. The Croydon line was a short one and enjoyed only a brief life of independence as it merged with the Brighton in 1846 to form the London, Brighton & South Coast Railway. It introduced several innovations in railway practice, however, which have ensured it a place in railway history. It had the world's first semaphore signal, the first signal box, a primitive form of interlocking points and signals, an experiment with atmospheric traction and the first railway flyover.

The C.M.G.R. closed in 1838, parts of its route being used for the construction of the Brighton line. The S.I.R. closed in 1846 and part of its route was later used for the line between Wimbledon and Croydon. Few traces remain of either railways or canal except for their influence on property boundaries; a short section of embankment and cutting of the C.M.G.R.; and a short stretch of the canal in Betts Park, Anerley and Norwood Lake which was the main reservoir for the canal.

Croydon,

SURREY.

To Coal Merchants, Lightermen, & Others.
Trading on the Croydon Canal.

TO BE

Sold by Auction,

(PEREMPTORILY,)

BY

Messrs. Blake,

AT THE CROYDON CANAL WHARF.

NORTH-END, CROYDON.

On WEDNESDAY, the 27th. JANUARY, 1819,

At ELEVEN for TWELVE o CLOCK

One Capital Canal

BARGE,

35 TONS.

May be Viewed till the Sale by applying to the Wharfinger at the Basin.

∴ Conditions of Sale as usual.

Printer, Croydon.

dd to Mr Edward pulland for £94.0.0

15. This auction notice has a handwritten note to the effect that the barge was sold for £94. The barges used on the Croydon Canal were not of the conventional pattern with living accommodation, as passage along the canal could be accomplished in one day.

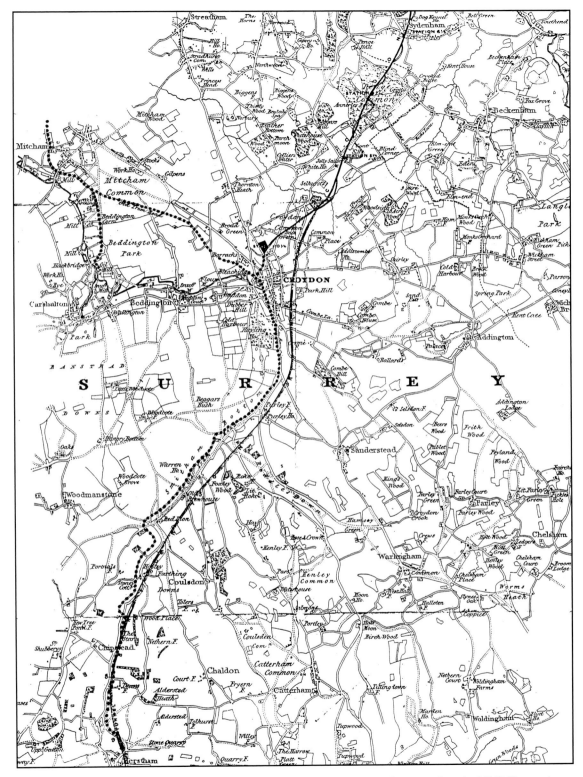

16.   Part of a map which was included in *The Croydon Railway and its Adjacent Scenery*, written by W. E. Trotter in 1839. The map shows the Brighton Railway, then under construction (no stations are indicated) and the alignment of the Surrey Iron and the Croydon, Merstham & Godstone Railways which are marked as 'Old Tram Road'. This has been highlighted here by means of dots to make it easier to follow. Several of the remaining sections of the canal can also be seen where the railway followed a more direct route.

CROYDON AND MERSTHAM IRON RAILWAY.

THE COMMITTEE of the CROYDON and MERSTHAM IRON RAILWAY COMPANY hereby give Notice, That the Railway from Croydon to Merstham is now open for the Use of the Public, on Payment of the following Tolls, viz.

For Dung .... 1d per Ton per Mile

For Limestone, Chalk, Lime, and all other Manure (except Dung) Clay, Breeze, Ashes, Sand, Bricks, Stone, Flints, and Fullers Earth .... } 2d per Ton per Mile

For Timber, Tin, Copper, Lead, Iron, Charcoal, Coke, Culm, Corn and Seeds, Flour, Malt, and Potatoes ...... } 3d per Ton per Mile

For Coals .... 3d per Chaldron per Mile

And for all other Goods .... 3d per Ton per Mile

By Order of the Committee,

W. B. LUTTLY,

Clerk of the Company.

Wandsworth, 8th January, 1805.

17. This card gives details of the tolls payable for use of the newly-opened Croydon, Merstham & Godstone Railway (which never actually reached Godstone). This and the Surrey Iron Railway were really one undertaking but had separate acts of parliament. It seems that the company provided the track and users provided their own wagons and horses.

18. The Brighton Railway is here shown under construction at Croydon, *c.*1840. The land on the left is now part of Coombe Cliff, and the bridge carrying Coombe Road is in the middle distance. Railway building was a highly labour-intensive operation and hundreds of navvies would be employed at any one time, usually staying in temporary camps, and sometimes causing trouble because of their unruly and drunken behaviour.

19. Neither the Surrey Iron nor the Croydon, Merstham & Godstone Railways had any major earthworks, but the latter did have several embankments and cuttings south of Croydon as it climbed into the North Downs. Views of the railways are rare, but this 1823 drawing by G. B. Wollaston shows a train crossing Chipstead Valley Road, near Smitham Bottom.

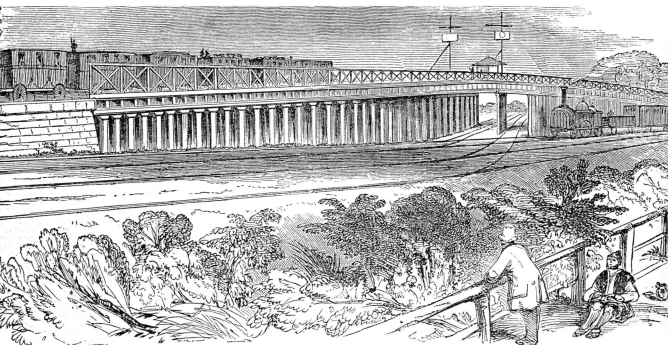

20. In the early 1840s, traffic over the London & Croydon Railway was growing rapidly and the company was also planning to extend its line to Epsom. There was increasing interest in another form of traction – atmospheric propulsion. It was decided to adopt this and an additional track was laid on the south side of the existing railway. The system consisted of a tube laid centrally between the rails. A piston, connected to the train, was pushed inside the tube by pumping air behind it, whilst a vacuum was created in front by sucking air out. Pumping stations were sited at three-mile intervals along the line. The tube was fitted with airtight flaps of leather and iron strips, lined with tallow.

It was not possible to have junctions on an atmospheric railway, and the wooden viaduct seen here was constructed to carry it over the Brighton line at Selhurst. This was probably the first segregated transport flyover in the world. The atmospheric railway opened between Forest Hill and Croydon in January 1846. Numerous problems arose and in July 1846 the Croydon and Brighton railways amalgamated to form the London, Brighton & South Coast Railway. Within six months it was decided to work the Epsom line as a conventional railway and the project was abandoned in May 1847.

CROYDON RAILWAY.

The Public are respectfully informed that on and after FRIDAY, the 1st of MAY, the Trains will start as follow, viz.—

DOWN TRAINS.
FROM TOOLEY STREET.

MORNING.	AFTERNOON.
5 minutes after 8	20 minutes after 4
5 minutes after 9	*20 minutes after 5
5 minutes after 10	
5 minutes after 11	* This Train meets the Reigate Coach at Croydon.
5 minutes after 12	
AFTERNOON.	20 minutes after 6
	20 minutes after 7
20 minutes after 2	20 minutes after 8
20 minutes after 3	20 minutes after 9

UP TRAINS.
FROM CROYDON.

MORNING.	AFTERNOON.
5 minutes after 8	20 minutes after 2
5 minutes after 9	~~20 minutes after 3~~
*5 minutes after 10	20 minutes after 4
	20 minutes after 5
* This Train is in communication with the Reigate Coach.	20 minutes after 6
	20 minutes after 7
5 minutes after 11	20 minutes after 8
5 minutes after 12	20 minutes after 9

Stopping at the intermediate Stations, viz.,—New Cross; Dartmouth Arms; Sydenham; Anerly, near Westow Hill, Norwood; and Jolly Sailor, near Beulah Spa, and that part of Norwood.

SUNDAYS,

The Trains will start as follow, calling at the intermediate Stations, viz.—

DOWN TRAINS.
FROM TOOLEY STREET.

MORNING.	AFTERNOON.
5 minutes after 8	20 minutes after 4
25 minutes before 9	10 minutes before 5
5 minutes after 9	20 minutes after 5
25 minutes before 10	10 minutes before 6
5 minutes after 10	20 minutes after 6
AFTERNOON.	20 minutes after 7
	10 minutes before 7
10 minutes before 2	20 minutes after 7
20 minutes after 2	10 minutes before 8
10 minutes before 3	20 minutes after 8
20 minutes after 3	10 minutes before 9
10 minutes before 4	20 minutes after 9

UP TRAINS.
FROM CROYDON.

MORNING.	AFTERNOON.
5 minutes after 8	20 minutes after 4
25 minutes before 9	10 minutes before 5
5 minutes after 9	20 minutes after 5
25 minutes before 10	10 minutes before 6
5 minutes after 10	20 minutes after 6
AFTERNOON.	10 minutes before 7
	20 minutes after 7
10 minutes before 2	10 minutes before 8
20 minutes after 2	20 minutes after 8
10 minutes before 3	10 minutes before 9
20 minutes after 3	20 minutes after 9
10 minutes before 4	

The Servants of the Company are prohibited receiving any Fee or Gratuity.

☞ **PARCELS may be BOOKED at ALL the above-named STATIONS.**

FARES.

	1st Class.	2nd Class.
London to New Cross	1s. 0d.	0s. 6d
— Dartmouth Arms	1 6	1 0
— Sydenham	1 6	1 0
— Anerly, near Westow Hill, Norwood	1 6	1 0

	1st Class.	2nd Class.
London to Jolly Sailor, near Beulah Spa, and that part of Norwood	1s. 6d.	1s. 0d
— Croydon	1 9	1 3

205, Tooley Street,
April 25, 1840.

R. S. YOUNG, SECRETARY.

** The Passage to and from London and Croydon is performed in about 30 Minutes; and Omnibusses meet every Train at the latter Station.

J. S. WRIGHT, PRINTER, CROYDON.

21. This 1840 timetable gives the first train as 8.05 a.m., which suggests that not many ordinary workers were expected to make use of the railway. There was a break of some two-and-a-quarter hours at lunchtime and even longer on Sundays, when trains were not permitted to run during the period of morning church services. The Sunday frequency was otherwise double that of weekdays, presumably to cater for pleasure traffic.

22. A gas-works was established at Butcher Row in 1827, by Messrs. Barnard and Defries. In 1829 the works was purchased by Henry Overton, the brewer. The Croydon, Merstham and Godstone Railway passed just to the rear of the works and no doubt the coal was brought in by the railway until its closure. This notice dates from the early days – probably the 1830s. In 1847 the works was taken over by the newly formed Croydon Commercial Gas and Coke Company.

23. The London & Croydon Railway Company was quick to see the potential for promoting leisure travel, as is demonstrated by this advertisement from one of the several contemporary booklets describing the scenery and details of construction of the line. Two of the stations, Dartmouth Arms and Jolly Sailor, took their names from adjacent hostelries on the canal. A few years later the former was renamed Forest Hill and the latter Norwood Junction. The canal had pursued a somewhat tortuous course in the Penge, Anerley and Norwood areas and a number of disconnected sections remained after the railway was built. Several of these saw use for leisure purposes for some years but were gradually filled in as their stagnant water became a nuisance and building development spread.

As the town grew, so better local administration was needed. The manor based on the palace had administered the town for centuries and although the inhabitants had petitioned for incorporation as a borough in 1691 and again in 1707, and royal approval had been given, for some reason a charter did not materialise. It is probable that the archbishop, as lord of the manor, prevented it to protect his privileges, especially income from the market. In any event, for some time the Vestry and (after 1819) the Select Vestry carried main responsibility for administering the affairs of the town, with the Surveyors responsible for the highways as they had been from Elizabethan times. In the early 19th century other bodies became involved as well. The Waste Land Trustees had duties that included supervision of the market, the town hall and burial arrangements, and from 1836 a Board of Guardians was responsible for the poor. From 1829 the Improvement Commissioners were concerned with street lighting, fire fighting, and for a short while a local paid police force. The Metropolitan Police took over responsibility for the latter in 1840. These bodies struggled with the increasing problems of a growing town until the Local Board of Health was established in 1849 and took over most of their duties, except for those related to the poor which remained with the Board of Guardians.

Croydon's location made its administration particularly difficult. Streams forming the main source of the River Wandle rose on the west side of the Brighton Road, flowed past the *Blue Anchor*, along Southbridge Road and through Old Town. They were there increased by spring water from Scarbrook and Laud's ponds, and they then fed into a large mill pond opposite the Parish Church. In these streams, trout had been caught until around the 1820s. A bourne, which also added considerably to the volume of water, came to the surface only intermittently, rising in the Caterham Valley and at Smitham Bottom. When it appeared, after a succession of wet seasons, flooding occurred on the Brighton Road and, more significantly, in the older low-lying parts of the town, sometimes lasting for five or six weeks and usually bringing fever and death. By the middle of the 19th century Croydon, in common with most expanding towns, was experiencing serious problems resulting from lack of proper drainage, sanitation and untainted water supplies. Conditions deteriorated as the inhabitants used the streams and ponds coincidentally as sewers and drainage ditches, and also as their source of water. Outbreaks of cholera, typhoid and other fevers were frequent.

In the face of national concern at such conditions, the Public Health Act was passed in 1848 enabling the setting up of local boards of health. These were intended to have comprehensive control over such matters as water supply, sewerage, drainage, cleansing, paving and burial. A public enquiry was held in the town in March 1849 by an inspecting civil engineer, William Ranger. His report of April 1849 highlighted the dreadful conditions then prevailing as these brief extracts show:

In the lower parts dense fogs prevail and hang upon the surface in the vicinity of Southbridge and Bog Island, whilst at and near Waddon there are marshes, with stagnant ditches from 12 to 15 feet wide charged with animal and vegetable matter from which noxious exhalations are conveyed by the prevailing winds to the town; moreover the town itself is entirely devoid of under-drainage and therefore dependent on a surface drainage, which is a source of unhealthy exhalations, giving rise to epidemics which have of late years greatly increased.

The inhabitants throw their sullage into the public drains in the street, not intended for that purpose; consequently the streets are constantly in a filthy state, and the drains still more so.

Those enormous reservoirs of filth, called Laud's and Scarbrook Ponds, have been used from time immemorial to receive the sullage of the town, as well as that from slaughterhouses and private dwellings. Laud's Pond is not only an abominable nuisance at all times, but must be the means of creating fevers and other diseases. The stench from it is very bad, and in the summer unbearable ... I think there are not more than 300 water-closets in the whole parish, the residue consisting of common privies, many of which are placed in situations regardless of ordinary decency and convenience, producing the most serious consequences to the inhabitants

It should be recalled that the population was by then nearly 20,000.

The average of privies among the poorer classes is not above one to three houses, many of these houses containing several families.
In several yards and courts at the south end of High Street and in the district of Southbridge, Pump Pail, Union Street, Mill Street and the Old Town generally ... the privies are all open, overhanging the water course and ... a child visiting such a place some time since fell through and was drowned.

A survey of well-water supplies showed that of the 1,550 houses in the parish:

775 are not supplied at all; 275 complain that the water is not good and the supply insufficient. The occupants of 14 houses are obliged to buy beer to get water from the landlord's pump; and in the Old Town, out of 213 houses, 143 are deficient in supply, and 24 find the water unfit for use.'

The report recommended the application of the Public Health Act to Croydon and it was one of the first 15 towns on which the powers of the Act were simultaneously conferred in August 1849. The election of members for the first Croydon Local Board of Health took place in the same month and it started work in September 1849 under the imaginative and innovative chairmanship of Cuthbert Johnson, a barrister, agricultural journalist and nationally-known figure in the public health field. Johnson continued in the position, with only one short break, until 1877.

Within two years the Board had planned and constructed a new waterworks pumping station in Surrey Street, a large underground reservoir at Park Hill, a sewage disposal works at Beddington and some miles of water mains and sewers. They had also removed the mill dam near the church, filled up all the ponds and ditches near the town centre, abolished cesspools and open privies, and provided 1,300 water closets in their place. Road drainage, new and improved footways and water supplies and sewer connections to 1,700 houses had also been installed.

These benefits were at first confined to a Special District which was the central part of the parish. The Lambeth Water Company meanwhile had in 1847 started to supply parts of Upper Norwood and in 1850 extended its supply to parts of South Norwood as well. Croydon had done its work so expeditiously that it was the first town to gain the benefits of public water supply and sewerage under the 1848 Public Health Act. Despite outbreaks of typhoid and numerous technical problems in the ensuing years, it soon achieved national prominence for its innovations and experiments in sanitary science.

By the year 1851 the foundations were well and truly laid for the tremendous expansion that the town was to experience in the future.

Parishioners of Croydon.

Church Rate.

Notice was given out in the Church on Sunday the 30th, of August, for a Vestry to be held on Tuesday Sept. the 8th 1812, for the purpose of making a new Church Rate— Have the arrears (£108) of the preceding Rates been collected?

This department of the Parish Assessment, Receipt, and Expenditure, is with the two Churchwardens only; one of whom is elected annually by the Parishioners, and the other appointed by the Minister.

A Vestry was held on the 11th, of August 1812, for the purpose of auditing the accounts of the Churchwardens of the preceding year 1811,--12.

It appears that this accounting of the Churchwards did not take place until four months after the end of their year,—The Law, directs it to be " *within a month after* " *at most*".

The Minister was not present at this accounting, the Law directs, that they (the Churchwardens) " shall, before the MINISTER and Parishioners, give up a just account "; Therefore the meeting of the Parishioners at the Church on the 11th, of August, did not constitute such a Vestry as the Law directs for the auditing of Churchwardens accounts, which requires the presence of the MINISTER.

The accounts being read, it appeared that the Churchwardens had carried to the account of the Church, the annual Rents of the Parish Estates.

Were these Estates intended for the benefit of the Church or for meliorating the condition of the Parish Poor?—To a question put to the Vicar's Churchwarden, who was presiding at the Vestry held for the purpose of auditing the Overseer's account of Poor's Rate for the year 1811--12, " *Out of what fund do you intend to pay the Vicar's* " *Parochial Rates, as voted to him at the Vestry on Easter Tuesday last* "? he answered, " *Out of the Parish Estates.*

Amongst the items of expenditure in the Churchwardens account 1811,--12, there appeared to be some that were connected with the Church, and tho' sanctioned by the vote of a Vestry, are certainly unauthorized by any existing Law—and others totally uncon-nected with the Church and its reparations, to which the expenditure of the Public Money is by Law limited.

Several of the items, as well as they could be noted down, during the reading the accounts were, as follows,

	£ : s : d
Paid over to Mr. Ward - - - - - - - -	4 : 14 : 0
Beadle Cleaning the Town Hall - - - -	2 : 2 : 0
Lighting Lamps about the Parish - - - -	15 : 1 : 0
Expenses at Visitation - - - - - - - -	7 : 11 : 0
Beadle's House and Goal - - - - - -	50 : 0 : 0
Expenses of Consecration - - - - - -	48 : 0 : 0
Rev. Mr. Price (Curate) - - - -	75 : 0 : 0
Easter Dinner - - - - - - - - -	10 : 0 : 0
Dinner for passing Accounts - - - - -	3 : 3 : 0
Work done at the Palace - - - - -	40 : 0 : 0
Mr. Ridley's Bill (Carpenter) - -	100 : 0 : 0
Mr. Castledine's Bill (ditto) - - -	17 : 0 : 0
Wine for Sacrament - - - - - - -	7 - 7 : 0
Parish Clerk's Bill - - - - - - - -	25 : 0 : 0
Parish Sexton's Bill - - - - - - - -	31 : 0 : 0
Repairing Chimes and Winding-up Clock &c. (two years) - - - - -	20 : 18 : 0
Blacksmith's Bill - - - - - - - -	6 : 7 : 0

Question? *What are the Debts Outstanding and Unpaid?*

24. This broadsheet published in 1812 suggests that discontent over rates and public expenditure is not just a feature of recent times.

CHILD FOUND.

TWO GUINEAS
REWARD.

Brought to the **WORKHOUSE** of the **CROYDON UNION**, **Duppa's Hill, Croydon, Surrey,** on the Evening of **MONDAY, th 23rd of SEPTEMBER, 1844,** about Nine o'Clock,

A FEMALE
INFANT CHILD,
AGED ABOUT ELEVEN MONTHS,

Rather small but pretty Features—very fair—Blue Eyes—Hair very light brown, inclining to red. It was dressed in a pink and white Print Frock with two frills round the arm—fine white Calico Petticoat— very good and clean Flannel Ditto, stitched round the bottom, with Calico Stays attached to it—Calico Chemise—white Cotton Socks— and black Slipper Shoes, buttoned round the ancle—had on a pale Blue Bonnet of Orleans Cloth. It has two teeth just through at the bottom, and two nearly through at the top. Was found last Evening after dusk in a Passage at WADDON, near CROYDON. It has evidently been used to Children, and in all probability to its Father, as it seems delighted with the former, and says "*Dada*," (the only word it can utter,) and goes readily and in preference to a gentleman. From these and other peculiarities it is supposed to have been STOLEN, and through fear of detection, has been left as above stated.

The above Reward will be given by the Guardians of the Croydon Union to any one who will give such information as will lead to the conviction of the person who so heartlessly abandoned the Child in manner above stated.

JAMES ANDREWS,
Clerk to the Guardians of the Croydon Union.

DUPPA'S HILL, CROYDON,
SEPTEMBER 24th, 1844.

25. Croydon's first workhouse was built on Duppas Hill in 1727. The Croydon Union and the Board of Guardians were established in 1836 by the Poor Law Commissioners under 1834 legislation. The Union comprised the parishes of Croydon, Addington, Coulsdon, Sanderstead, Woodmansterne, Beddington, Wallington, Mitcham, Merton, Morden and Penge. Conditions in the workhouse were harsh and the dread of going there clouded the lives of most poorer people. A new building was provided at Queen's Road in 1865 and in 1930 Croydon Council took over the functions of the Board of Guardians. Even at that time the regulations required anybody admitted to be searched, any money or valuables to be taken for safe-keeping, and all inmates to be in bed by 9.00 p.m. in summer and 8.00 p.m. in winter.

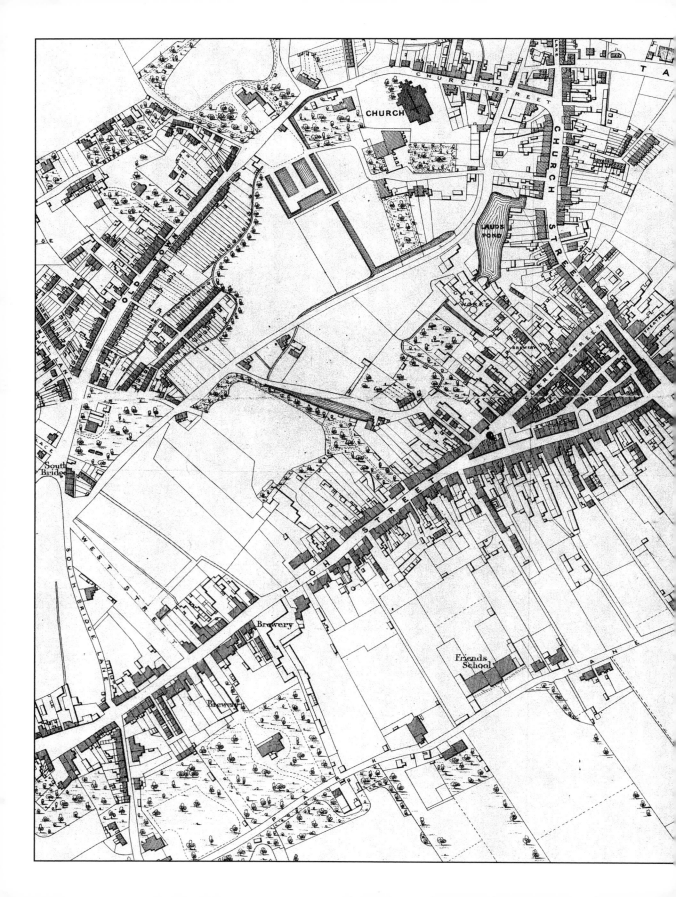

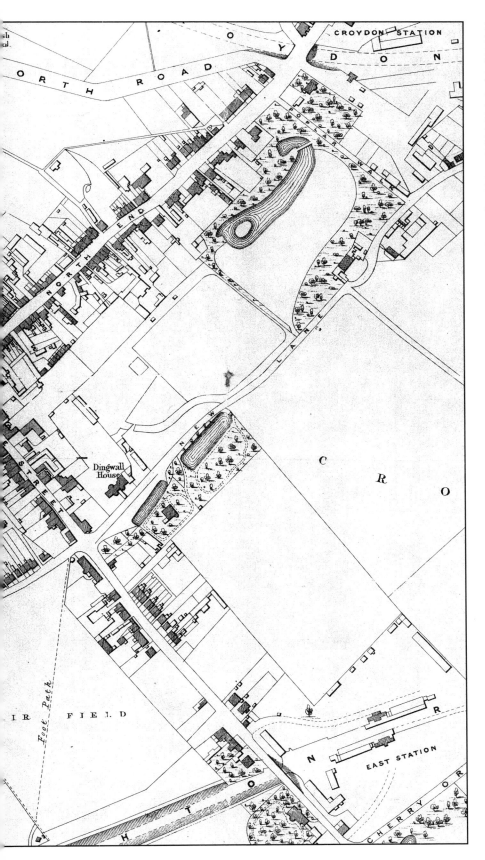

26. Part of W. Roberts'
map of the town in 1847,
prepared for the Tithe
Commissioners. North is
towards the top right corner.
The separate development of
the Old Town area near the
parish church is shown
clearly, as are the numerous
ponds and streams. The
distance between High
Street/North End and Park
Lane/New Lane is
approximately a furlong (a
furrow long) and it is
thought that these roads
were originally tracks
bounding the common
fields. Note the numerous
yards between High Street
and Park Lane, several of
them belonging to inns.
There were already two
railway stations, the more
important known simply as
Croydon, with the East
station set amongst the fields
in Addiscombe Road.

Urban Sprawl

27. The Waldrons, originally part of the Haling Park Estate, was bought by Edward Vigars who, in 1850 started selling plots to gentlemen who could employ their own architects to build houses. It was laid out as a private estate with two ornate lodges where green-liveried gate-keepers in top hats controlled access. This photograph was taken *c*.1862 from 15 The Waldrons looking south-east across the recently laid out garden and the fields towards South End. Beyond is the tower of St Peter's church, before the spire was added in 1864. The line of trees and hedges in the centre is approximately where Bramley Hill was developed soon afterwards. Note the well-wooded nature of the area at that time.

28. The beginning of the valley in which the old town stands is here seen from the high ground of Duppas Hill Terrace, *c*.1865. Some of the buildings in Old Town are in the foreground. Over the roofs to the left are the bleaching grounds of the Palace which at this time was being used as a factory. The field was formerly known as Great Palace Mead. On the right is the roof of the newly-built Whitgift 'Poor' School in Church Road, while the High Street is on the rising ground beyond. There were still many trees at this time which maintained the country town appearance.

The 1851 Census records the population of Croydon as 20,343. The adjacent parishes of Coulsdon, Sanderstead and Addington had only 713, 235 and 615 respectively. By 1931, the year of the last census before the Second World War, Croydon's population had reached 233,032, Coulsdon's 28,423, Sanderstead's 9,279 and Addington's 2,791. Further increases continued in the 1930s, particularly in Coulsdon, Sanderstead and Addington.

With improved water supply, sanitation and drainage, Croydon was ripe for expansion by the 1850s. The other parishes, remote from railway lines and high up on the North Downs, were to remain rural well into the 20th century. The new railways provided the opportunity for people to live further from the city than hitherto, whilst continuing to work there. Croydon, set in some of the most attractive countryside so close to London, was an obvious choice for residence. By 1861 its population had risen to 30,240, increasing rapidly to 55,652 by 1871, 78,953 by 1881; and reaching 102,795 by 1891.

Initially the new residents of Croydon consisted largely of prosperous merchants, clerks, tradesmen attracted to the growing town, domestic servants, and agricultural workers who drifted down from the hills and in from the surrounding country to find jobs such as cab-drivers, grooms and railwaymen. As a rule the better, detached housing was on the higher land as at Park Hill, the Waldrons and Upper Norwood, whilst the lower and flatter areas were increasingly covered by smaller semi-detached or terraced houses. Sometimes, as in Parsons Mead, it happened gradually; sometimes it was almost overnight, as in Napier Road and Barrack Town.

Some of the new housing was of very poor quality. In 1864 Dr. Alfred Carpenter told the Local Board of Health that recently built working-class houses in the town had their walls plastered with mortar whose chief ingredients were common garden mould and scrapings off the roads, and the fumes given off sometimes killed the occupants. There were no by-laws to prevent the use of such ingredients nor even to prevent tenants from tearing away the skirting boards and even the banisters for use as firewood, nor to deter them from keeping horses, donkeys and other animals in their homes – occasional happenings in the poorer districts well into the 20th century.

To serve the needs of the growing populace, new churches, chapels, schools, corner shops, beer houses and inns, laundries, factories and small workshops appeared all over the town. But they were still interspersed with market gardens, fields and some large houses in extensive grounds which gradually succumbed to the builder as the owners died or moved to quieter places away from the ever encroaching tide of bricks and mortar.

But who were the developers? For the most part it was local men and local money (often the profits of shopkeepers) that changed the town; certainly until the 1920s. Many of the developments were small-scale, consisting of just a few houses or one street or even a single terrace of cottages. Some of the development was very cheaply built (e.g. Forster and Wilford roads which became known as Bang Hole) and some localities failed to attract the kind of people for whom the initial expensive housing was intended. In several instances the opening of a new railway station helped to stimulate new building as in the case of the district then called New Thornton Heath. Built by the Englishman's Freehold Land Society between the newly-opened station and the Norwood Hills, it consisted of small houses intended for purchase by the less well-off.

The building of the tramways and later expansion of motor bus routes also had their effect on the spread of building. Thus the tide gradually spread along the valleys to the south of the town centre and then up on to the slopes of the Downs, and northwards to meet the outward spread of London. By 1939 much of Croydon was built up, but with a few of the old estates surviving to the east, and as parks. There were, too, some remaining fragments of the Great North Wood, golf courses, allotments, and playing fields, several farms, some woodland and, to the south, open downland to break up the rows of houses. The transformation from small country town to large urban centre was virtually complete.

29. Addiscombe Place, photographed here c.1859, replaced an earlier house in about 1701. The walls and ceilings were decorated with many paintings of mythological subjects – some thought to have been the work of Sir James Thornhill. John Evelyn visited the place in 1703 (his son-in-law, William Draper owned it) and pronounced it 'to be one of the very best gentlemen's houses in Surrey, when finished'. In the late 18th century the estate was leased to Lord Hawkesbury, who was later created Earl of Liverpool, and was Prime Minister. He made it his principal residence. King George III and William Pitt often visited him at Addiscombe.

In 1808, Lord Liverpool died and the estate was bought by the Honourable East India Company which inaugurated here a military training college for their cadets, some of whom are in the picture. The college opened in 1809 and was soon extended. Up to 150 cadets at a time could be accommodated. Many stories are recorded of escapades involving cadets and local townspeople, and Croydon roughs used to waylay and ill-treat any cadet who ventured alone into the town. Well-known men who received their training at Addiscombe included Major-General Sir Henry Lawrence, Lord Napier of Magdala, and Lord Roberts of Kandahar. In 1861, following the Indian Mutiny, the company's military organisation was disbanded and Woolwich and Sandhurst were considered adequate for all requirements for officer training. Addiscombe College closed in August of that year and was sold to the British Land Company.

The mansion and most of the buildings were pulled down and the five roads named Canning, Clyde, Elgin, Havelock and Outram were constructed on the site; although having Indian connections, none of those named was educated at Addiscombe. This was one of the earliest examples of a substantial estate in the area being sold for large-scale development.

30. Following the Great Exhibition of 1851, the Crystal Palace was rebuilt just beyond the Croydon boundary at Penge Place, and opened in 1854. The new building was on a much enlarged scale and the grounds were magnificently landscaped. The lamp-post in the middle of the road in this 1898 view was on the site of the Vicar's Oak, an important boundary tree which had formerly marked the meeting point of the parishes of Lambeth, Camberwell, Battersea (Penge), and Croydon.

The Crystal Palace stimulated the growth of the surrounding districts, and Upper Norwood with its fine views expanded as large houses in spacious grounds covered much of the area. The development of that part of Croydon was totally separate from most of the remainder of the parish, where building gradually spread out from the town centre. The huge bulk of the Crystal Palace was a local landmark, and its many attractions were a great draw for 80 years until its destruction by fire in 1936.

UPPER·NORWOOD
AND·CRYSTAL·PALACE
EXCEPTIONALLY·HEALTHY
BECAUSE·OF·PREVAILING
WIND·FROM·THE·COAST

380·FEET·ABOVE·THAMES·THEREFORE
OUT·OF·THE·VALLEY·FOGS
THE·FRESH·AIR·SUBURB

31. The Upper Norwood area was rather imaginatively, but perhaps not too accurately, promoted by this advertisement of about 1900.

32 - 34. Opened in 1831, the Royal Beulah Spa and Gardens enjoyed only a short existence, its closure in 1858 being hastened by the counter attractions of the Crystal Palace erected in 1854 only about a mile away. Designed by the famous architect, Decimus Burton, the features included a camera obscura, a maze, a circus ring, two lakes, the spa-well and a refreshment room. Events included dancing, archery, fortune-telling, firework displays and ballooning. Tivoli Lodge (centre background) still stands on the corner of Spa Hill and Beulah Hill. Much of the site, including some of its woodland, is now the Lawns open space. The octagon, seen through the trees to the right of the contemporary print, survived for many years, and the photograph of it dates from around 1900.

ROYAL
BEULAH SPA
NORWOOD.

ANOTHER
GRAND FÊTE
AL FRESCO,
On Thursday next, Aug. 18, 1836,

On which occasion the following Entertainments will take place, in addition to the usual Amusements of the Gardens:—

THE CELEBRATED

Grotesque Dancers

Mr. GIBSON, Mr. KING, and Mr. BROWN, assisted by MRS. GIBSON, Miss DAVIES, and Miss SMITHSON, will dance, in character,

A Chinese Comic Dance--A Comic Bedouin Arab Dance, and an Old English May-pole Morris Dance, as danced by them at the *Duchess of St. Alban's* Fête Champêtre, and for which purpose a MAY-POLE, beautifully decorated will be erected in the centre of the Lawn.

A Concert in the **Rustic Orchestra,** by MRS. FITZWILLIAM, the MISSES DUNN, MESSRS. FITZWILLIAM, HOBBS, HAWKINS, and ATKINS.

The Celebrated Mr. HARPER, of the King's Theatre, will play the VOICE PART of the *'Soldier Tired'* upon the **Trumpet,** and accompany the Misses DUNN in various Songs.

Duetts on the Royal Kent Bugle by Messrs. CALVERT and JONES.

Ramo Samee & his Infant Daughter will exhibit their astonishing Performances.

A grand ARCHERY MEETING, when various Prizes will be contended for, and in which the Visitors are invited to participate.

The Rosery and Lawn will be tastefully inclosed for **Public Dancing,** under the superintendence of a Professor of Eminence.

A Full Military Band, under the direction of Mr. WOOD.

Miechel's German Band.

The Surrey Yeomanry Band, conducted by Mr. WALLACE.

Refreshments may be obtained at the Confectionary on the Grounds.

35. Norbury Farm photographed here *c.*1906, was thought to be the original mansion house of the Manor of Norbury, first recorded in 1229. The farmhouse demonstrates the fairly common practice in this area of using wood for building purposes. It stood approximately where Kensington and Norbury Avenues now meet and was demolished in 1914.

36. In 1493 Green Lane was described as the way leading from the Hermitage to Whitehorse. It was certainly an ancient highway, as is demonstrated by the mature hedges and trees seen in this postcard view of *c.*1907. The road was widened, and housing covered this and most of the remaining open land in the north of the borough during the 1920s and 1930s.

37. Looking north along London Road, Thornton Heath in 1907; the road on the left is Dunheved Road North. Large houses had been built in the late 19th century and most of those on the right had carriage entrances. Note the splendid railings and gates. This part of London Road looks much less attractive today. All the houses on the right have gone, as have most of the trees.

38. Originally Beulah Road West, then Beulah Road North, this Thornton Heath street photographed *c*.1906 was renamed Burlington Road in 1902. There are several distinct designs of house in this short section of the road and the larger Victorian houses on the higher ground of Norwood can be seen beyond.

39. Dixon Road, South Norwood was cut through the grounds of The Elms in the late 1920s. With Nugent and Elm Park Roads, and some houses fronting on to Whitehorse Lane, the new development was known as the Elm Park Estate and had its own tennis club for residents. This photograph dates from *c*.1930. The road surface was as yet unmetalled and the tradesmen were still using horse-drawn delivery vehicles, as they would for another 20 years or more.

40. Thornton Heath Pond, photographed *c*.1936, was formerly a large cattle pond and well-known landmark. The fountain was provided by local residents to mark the Golden Jubilee of Queen Victoria's reign in 1887. The pond survived until 1953 when it was filled in and a small garden provided in what is now a traffic roundabout.

41.   Locally-made bricks were used in most of the new houses in the area. The London clay of north Croydon was particularly suitable for brick-making and there were brick fields at Norbury, Whitehorse Lane, Clifton Road, Portland Road, Morland Road and Woodside in addition to Thomas Pascall's Brick Field and Pottery, photographed here in 1866. This was at South Norwood High Street. The key to the letters is only partially complete. A is the railway signal box at Goat House Bridge, C is the house next to the railway at Sunny Bank, and H marks houses in the High Street. The long low structures appear to be drying sheds. The last local brickworks at Woodside did not close until 1974.

42.   Contrary to popular belief, not all speculative housing ventures in the Victorian or subsequent periods were successful. These houses on the southern side of Eldon Park at South Norwood, together with another group of nine, were built by Gregory and Daynes. Work started in 1857 but was never completed and they became known locally as 'the Carcases'. They were demolished in 1897.

43. Electric trams reached Addiscombe in 1902 but there was then little housing in the immediate vicinity of the terminus, seen here *c*.1906. The horse trams originally ran on beyond this point to South Norwood, but as most of the route went through open country the line operated only for a few years, and subsequently only on race days to serve the racecourse at Woodside. The railway bridge carried the Woodside & South Croydon Railway which was for some years run jointly by the London, Brighton & South Coast and the South Eastern & Chatham railways – each company providing the trains for one year at a time. The electric trams undoubtedly encouraged new housing in the district which was fairly well built up by the 1920s.

44. This advertising postcard shows 2 to 10 Inglis Road, Addiscombe, *c*.1906. It has the following printed on the back: 'WHY PAY RENT for years and in the end be no better off, when you can purchase your own house by paying a small deposit of £25 down and balance can be arranged on a repayable Mortgage? This is one of the best investments ever offered to the public. Before writing call and view these Villas in Inglis and Sundridge Roads, Addiscombe Tram Terminus. Price – Freehold, £375, or Leasehold, £275, at £5 Ground Rent. Containing Three Bedrooms; Bath room, hot and cold; and W.C.; Drawing-room, Dining-room, Kitchen and Scullery combined. Apply LEADER, Builder on Estate'.

45.   Formerly part of Ham Farm, this area was developed from the early 1920s, the early roads all following the alignment of existing farm tracks, and building taking place in a haphazard manner. This postcard view, sent in 1923, is looking north along The Glade, approximately from where Greenview Avenue was later built on the right. The bungalow in the distance is now 149 and 149A The Glade. The message on the back of the postcard is: 'My land runs right through the wood seen in the distance. Saw rabbits and a pheasant in my part of the wood on Saturday last – Percy'.

46.   Sand pits were recorded at Shirley early in the 18th century, and the workers settled on Shirley Common in the area known as Badger's Hole, photographed here in 1907. The single-storey cottages were demolished c.1935-6 but the other houses mostly remain. The boundary between Croydon and Addington parishes was approximately where the children are standing. The open heather-clad hills are often referred to as Shirley Hills although their correct name is Addington Hills. Following the purchase of part by the Local Board of Health in 1874, the remainder was acquired by Croydon Corporation in three stages between 1903 and 1919. With an area of 130 acres, reaching a height of 460 ft. (125 m.) above sea level, and giving extensive views over Croydon and London, the hills became a popular resort for organised parties and Sunday school treats. Local villagers even took in paying guests from south London during the summer. Shirley gained its first chapel in 1856, but it remained a country village until the extensive housing development of the 1920s and '30s. It still retains large areas of open space, although farming ceased in the 1950s.

47.   William Webb, a partner in the local estate agents, Hooker and Webb, started laying out his ideal estate of 260 acres off Foxley Lane in 1888. Trees, shrubs and hedges were planted and the roads were metalled before the first house was completed in 1903. A village green and the *Lord Roberts* temperance inn seen here *c*.1908 completed the rural illusion. The building also served as post office and village stores, as it still does today. The crowds used to come by tram for a pleasant Sunday afternoon stroll through this excellent example of early garden city type development, but the pond has long since been filled in and the *Lord Roberts* no longer serves teas.

48.   Sanderstead church is situated high on the Downs, nearly 570 ft. (155 m.) above sea level. The earliest reference to it is in a ninth-century Saxon charter. The church dates from the 13th century. Sanderstead Court, alongside, was built in 1676 but was demolished in 1958. The village consisted of a few scattered houses and a shop, but there was never a public house. The opening of the Croydon, Oxted & East Grinstead Railway in 1884, and a station called Sanderstead, in reality over a mile away, and some 300 ft. (80 m.) down the hill nearer Croydon, led to some housing development in the lower parts. This view was taken in the early 1920s and it was not until the 1930s that the hill-top settlement saw any really significant changes.

49. Viewed from the chalk cliff above the recently rebuilt station in 1900, Foxley Lane (centre) already had a few houses, but otherwise open downland stretched away into the distance. Note the flint walls forming field boundaries in the right background. Purley station had opened in 1841 as Godstone Road, but had then closed in 1847 as the area was almost completely devoid of population. With the opening of the branch line to Caterham in 1856, it was reopened as Caterham Junction and in 1881 was renamed Purley.

50. Selsdon was formerly a detached part of Croydon Parish, known as Croydon Crook. In 1883, when Croydon achieved borough status, Selsdon became part of Sanderstead parish. Selsdon House was the principal building in the area which was otherwise farm and woodland. The house became the *Selsdon Park Hotel* in 1925. The area remained rural until the establishment of a large number of smallholdings after the First World War, and the housing development of the 1920s and '30s which completely changed its character. This view, dating from *c.*1922, is from approximately where Lynne Close now stands, towards Selsdon Wood which became a National Trust property in 1936.

51. Looking north along the Brighton Road at Smitham Bottom in 1906. Lion Green Road with the gates and lodge of Cane Hill Hospital are on the left. The building in the fork of the roads was Coppard's temperance hotel, for many years a popular refreshment place for cyclists on the Brighton Road. The bare slopes of the almost treeless Downs were as yet hardly touched by builders. As the area came to be built up it became known as Coulsdon, and the original settlement on the Downs became known as Old Coulsdon. The local station on the Tattenham Corner line is still called Smitham.

52. By the time this aerial view postcard was published in 1934, the village was known as Old Coulsdon. St John's, the parish church dating from *c.*1260, is on the extreme right, with Coulsdon Road running across the centre of the picture, and a 409 bus just visible in front of the newly-built Purley County Grammar School. It was unusual for a school, especially a grammar school, to open before most of the new development had taken place. Tudor Parade, the local shops, is mid-way between the church and school, and in the view a haystack stands where the *Tudor Rose* car park is today. Coulsdon had remained virtually unchanged until Edmund Byron of Coulsdon Court, squire for 58 years, died in 1921, and the estate was broken up. By 1939 the area had been extensively developed for housing.

Town Centre and Shopping

In 1851 most of Croydon's shops were located in the town centre, principally in Church Street, High Street, South End, and the market area. Otherwise there were just a few, mainly serving local needs in South and Upper Norwood, around Thornton Heath Pond and at Broad Green.

With the arrival of the railway in the 19th century the markets began to decline in importance. But as the town grew, so did the number, variety and quality of shops in its centre. The better shops would even arrange to serve customers whilst they sat outside in their carriages, and many would deliver purchases.

The market triangle formed by Surrey Street, Crown Hill and High Street was already much run down by 1851, although many of the buildings were of great antiquity and should have been an asset to the town. The population of the small 'core' was already 449 but had risen to 590 by 1861, with on average 11 persons to a house. Nearly half of the houses in the streets and alleys were common lodging houses, each containing an average of 24 people. Many of the lodgers were prostitutes and, as the century wore on, the position deteriorated still further. Charles 'Uncle' Day controlled 20 of the 28 lodging houses existing at the time of his death in 1892. He also had similar properties in Kingston. The *Croydon Chronicle*, in 1888, described his properties as 'a human moral piggery that for low depravity, either Newcastle or Manchester might match, but certainly could not surpass'.

The High Street too was a problem, being very narrow and a source of constant congestion and complaint. Even the new town council, established in 1883, found that there were no easy solutions especially as many wealthy and influential local residents, mostly conservative, liked the 'quaintness' of the place and did not want an increase in the rates to modernise it. The tradesmen, mostly liberal, did want improvements. Eventually the Croydon Improvement Act was passed in 1890. This enabled the Council to acquire land in the triangle compulsorily and then lease, sell or exchange it. Fortunately the Council was able at the same time to buy the site of the recently closed Central railway station and build on the site a new town hall, thereby releasing the site of the old one in the High Street and facilitating road widening there.

Demolition of what had become Croydon's 'Red Light District' started in June 1893 and by 1896 the new Town Hall was open in Katharine Street, the market triangle had mostly been cleared and the High Street had been widened. By that time North End and George Street also contained a number of shops and these were still increasing. Meanwhile as houses spilled over the surrounding fields and woods, so corner shops, small shopping parades and quite substantial local shopping centres became established.

By the time of the Second World War the town centre had three large department stores and numerous other excellent shops, but in relation to its population the commercial area was perhaps somewhat smaller than might have been expected. However, this was to change dramatically with the redevelopment of the 1960s, as was the general style of shopping.

53. Croydon's market would originally have been an open space but, as in many towns, rows of temporary stalls were gradually replaced by permanent structures and it is to this, no doubt, we owe the names Butcher and Middle Rows. Old deeds refer to a fish market and this was probably situated near the junction of Middle and Market Streets, just behind the photographer. In this illustration of *c.*1890 the women are standing outside the shop of Anthony Cooper, tripe dresser, 2 Market Street.

    The maternal grandmother of John Ruskin, the eminent Victorian, was at one time landlady of the *King's Head* in Market Street, and his mother's sister married George Richardson, a baker of Market Street, a few doors along on the left. John Ruskin has left the following description of his childhood visits: '... But whenever my father was ill – and hard work and sorrow had already set their mark on him – we all went down to Croydon to be petted by my homely aunt; and walk on Duppas Hill and on the heather of Addington. My aunt lived in the little house still standing – or which was so four months ago – the fashionablest in Market Street, having actually two windows over the shop, in the second storey, but I never troubled myself about the superior part of the mansion, unless my father happened to be making drawings in Indian ink, when I would sit reverently by and watch; my chosen domain being at all other times the shop, the bakehouse, and the stones around the spring of crystal water at the back door (long since let down into the modern sewer) ...'. This reference to the springs is a reminder of why Croydon grew up where it did. Unfortunately by Victorian times much of the water had become polluted.

    The whole of the market area became known generally as Middle Row in later days.

54. Looking along Middle Street *c*.1890, Streeter's Hill is to the right and left, and in the distance is Bell Hill which at that time linked Surrey Street and High Street. The small opening straight ahead led to Crown Hill. The wood-clad building just to the left of the archway still exists in the remaining short section of Bell Hill. The Cherry Fair, established by Archbishop Stratford in 1343, was apparently held in the market area but it seems that a child was killed by a swing in the 1840s and this, together with the nuisance created in a congested area, may have hastened its abolition.

55. This photograph of Streeter's Hill appears to date from 1893, just before demolition of the Middle Row area, for the buildings are mostly boarded up and some have broken windows. The *Prince of Wales* beer house is on the left, on the corner of Market Street. Middle Street runs across the centre.

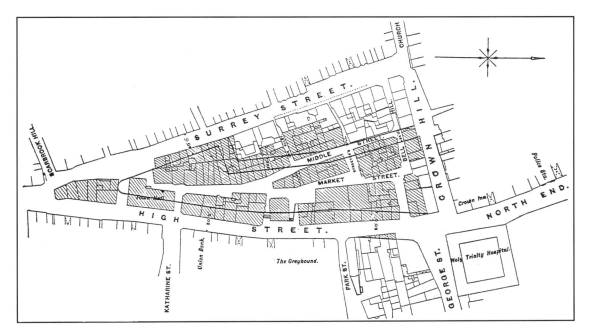

56.   This plan of the proposed improvements to the market area was published in the *Croydon Advertiser* of 5 October 1889. All the buildings shaded on the plan were eventually demolished. The new frontages and the line of the new Middle Street are shown by solid black lines.

57.   In 1883 the sign of the *Greyhound* still stretched across the High Street which was only about 25 ft. (8 m.) wide between the buildings. The *Greyhound* was formerly the town's principal inn and dated from the 15th century or earlier. On the left is the former Butter Market, built in 1807, and at this time used as offices by the *Croydon Chronicle*. All the buildings on the left were demolished so that the High Street could be widened in the early 1890s under the improvement scheme.

58. An impressive array of four- and five-storey buildings was erected on the west side of the High Street to replace those seen in illustration 57. The Grant brothers from Devon who had started a small drapery shop opposite, in 1877, moved into part of the new buildings (on the left) and their business later expanded to become one of the town's three large department stores. It remained a family business until the early 1980s, and the store later closed. The *Greyhound* (right) disappeared in a redevelopment in the 1960s. The widening of the street allowed the southern and northern sections of the horse tramway to be joined and in 1901 the electric trams started running, as seen in this view, *c.*1906.

59.   Katharine Street was laid out in 1866 when the Central railway station was constructed. In this 1890 view, the second Town Hall in the High Street can be seen in the distance, with the cutting and railway station behind the wall and fence on the left. The station, a terminus at the end of what must have been the shortest branch line in the country, opened in 1868, closed in 1871, re-opened in 1886 and closed finally in 1890. The site was then purchased by the Corporation and the third Town Hall was built there, with gardens in the cutting. The offices of the Croydon Gas Company are just visible on the right.

60. 4 George Street is representative of a number of private houses remaining in the town centre in the 19th century, and was photographed in 1866, when it was occupied by George Cooper, a surgeon. In the left background is the Whitgift schoolmaster's house, built in 1600 just after completion of the almshouses. The original school was adjacent. The houses and school were demolished in 1897; Allders now occupies the site. There appears to be an early example of graffiti on the right-hand gate of no. 4.

61. Looking along George Street towards East Croydon station, from the corner of Park Lane, c.1906. On the left are the Public Halls. Erected by the Croydon Literary and Scientific Institution in 1860, the building was the venue for many social events and leisure activities. In 1929 it was bought by Croydon Corporation and was demolished in the late 1950s. The income from the redeveloped site was used to help fund the construction of the Fairfield Halls. The clock in the tower of Thrift's wholesale grocery warehouse came from the second Town Hall. This part of George Street was widened and almost completely rebuilt during the redevelopment of the 1960s.

62. Crown Hill was named after the inn which stood at the junction with North End, opposite the Whitgift Hospital. This 1908 postcard view is notable for the large number of advertisements, including a suggestion that one should 'eat chocolate, and keep well'. The Croydon Hippodrome on the right was opened in 1867 as the Theatre Royal, but the site had formerly been used for an earlier theatre. The Hippodrome became a cinema and was the first in the town to show talking pictures, in 1929.

63.   North End c.1880, with Crown Hill and the *Crown Hotel* on the left and Whitgift Hospital and George Street to the right. Next to the hospital is the *Swan Inn*, demolished c.1889 for an extension to Joshua Allder's adjoining shop. One of the town's first Aldermen, Allder was also Chairman of the Croydon Tramways Company. It is reputed that he employed one of his handymen from the shop to check tickets on the trams from time to time. Allders is now the third largest department store in the country.

64. This advertisement from Warren's Croydon Directory for 1865-6 is a reminder of a shop which was started in 1769 by John Harris from Streatham. The firm of Hammond & Purrott later became Hammond & Hussey. The shop stood, virtually unaltered from that shown in the drawing, in the High Street next to the *Greyhound*, until demolition in the early 1960s. The extensive yard and outbuildings reached back to Park Lane and the site is now in St George's Walk.

65. Busy Surrey Street has long attracted shoppers as this view taken in the early 1930s shows. Until the 1840s, Surrey Street was known as Butcher Row; the 18th-century butcher's shop occupied by J. H. Roff & Sons (left) and adjacent properties were formerly part of a much longer terrace known as The Shambles. This was partly demolished in the late 1920s for an extension of Grant's store. The upper storeys extend out over the pavement and are supported on wooden posts – a rare survival in this part of Surrey.

66. In 1802 the Vestry considered a Resolution of the Court of Quarter Sessions concerning the need to provide a proper place of confinement for prisoners during the Assizes, the existing cage being inadequate. It appears that several influential local gentlemen raised sufficient funds by public subscription to construct a building to house a new gaol and accommodation for the beadle, in Butcher Row. This was then leased to the parish for £50 per annum for 60 years. By the mid-19th century the building was used as a corn warehouse, with cells below, but in 1861 alterations were made to the Town Hall and cells were provided there instead. The gaol then continued in use as a warehouse and shop, as it was when photographed here c.1937. It was demolished in 1957.

67. This view from the tower of the parish church dates from about 1908. J. L. Pearson's fine St Michael's church built in 1881 is in the centre background, with Lower Church Street and Reeves' Corner in the foreground. Apart from a few old buildings in the immediate vicinity of the church, most of those seen here had been erected after the mid-19th century.

68. Broad Green *c.*1913, looking north along London Road from the corner of Sumner Road. As the town grew, local shopping centres developed to serve the needs of the various districts. Broad Green is an almost continuous extension of the town centre but until the mid-19th century was little more than a few cottages and the *Half Moon* public house. Because of the busy nature of the London to Brighton road, most of the premises between Broad Green and the *Swan & Sugar Loaf*, a distance of nearly two miles, were by 1900 being used for commercial purposes.

69.   The Cosy Dining Rooms at 18 High Street,
South Norwood was owned by the Croydon Coffee
Tavern Company Ltd. It describes itself as 'the best
pull up for carmen in Croydon'. With an opening
time of 5.30 a.m. the staff no doubt worked very
long hours. Judging by their appearance, a fairly
superior class of carman was catered for, possibly
too superior as it seems to have survived for only
about two years from 1898 to 1900.

70.   Kennards department store grew from a
small, and not very successful, drapery business
started by William Kennard at North End in 1852.
By the 1930s the store could claim to be the largest
in the town and offered numerous attractions for
children of all ages, including pony rides and a zoo.
Here, in 1943, the store proudly advertised the
'largest Father Christmas in the world', weighing
43 stone and with a girth of 6 ft. 8 in. (2 m.) round
the waist. Debenhams store and the Drummond
Centre now occupy the site of Kennards.

71.   It was not uncommon in Victorian and Edwardian days for a butcher to lay on extravagant displays of poultry for Christmas. Indeed, meat and poultry were almost always displayed, not very hygienically, outside the shop. Here T. Goddard, dairyman of 164-6 Cherry Orchard Road, near the *Leslie Arms*, had mounted a splendid display for Christmas 1909, and was advertising a guessing competition for the number of birds displayed. The first prize was a 12 lb. turkey, the second a 10lb. goose, and the third a 4 lb. fowl. Nearly 600 birds were on show and the staff must have had a huge task in setting up the display, which was over 20 ft. (6 m.) high.

72. By 1800 Norwood was a hamlet developing into a small village, but it was not until the Crystal Palace came in 1854 that it experienced much growth. By 1900 it was a select district with good shops in Westow Hill, Westow Street, and Church Road. This view of Westow Hill *c.*1912 how the south tower of the Crystal Palace dominated the local scene.

73. This photograph was taken *c.*1927 in London Road, Norbury, looking towards Streatham. Northborough Road is to the left and the Norbury Cinema, opened in 1911 as the Palais de Luxe, and closed in 1937 after a somewhat chequered career, is immediately to the left of the bus. The shopping parades at Norbury developed from around 1901, when the electric trams reached there from Croydon.

74. Addington village, three and a half miles from the town centre, was still completely rural until the late 1930s. There was just one shop which opened in 1881 as a co-operative enterprise, and from 1884 also served as the post office. In this postcard view, sent in 1906, it also seems to have been a welcome haven providing refreshment for ramblers and cyclists. The shop ceased to be a co-operative between the wars and closed in the 1960s.

75. The Post Office and Village Stores was the only shop in Coulsdon before the housing development of the late 1920s and early 1930s. Here Mrs. Jeffry is proudly displaying her new pension book in 1908. She was the first inhabitant of the village to receive a state pension when introduced that year. It amounted to 5s. a week at the age of 70 if other earnings did not exceed 10s. a week. Mrs. Jeffry lived at the little round house at Bradmore Green, where she was lodge-keeper for The Grange, the house next to St John's church.

At Work

Local people could find employment in agriculture, small workshops and factories, domestic service, shops and transport. Hours were long and conditions were poor compared with today, and there was no security. Sundays and, from 1871, Bank Holidays, provided the only respite, but improvements came gradually as the 19th century progressed, with an early closing day for shops, and eventually paid holidays.

Agriculture and related activities were the prime local source of trade until the early 20th century. Sheep were grazed on the Downs while corn, barley and hops were grown widely and market gardens flourished to the north. In the fields to the west towards Wallington, Carshalton and Mitcham, lavender and herb growing thrived, with peppermint much used for medicinal purposes and it was not until 1949 that the distillery in Mitcham Road closed. Watercress too was a speciality of the headwaters of the River Wandle. As housing spread over the district so these activities diminished but the town increasingly became a centre for the wholesale meat trade.

With a profusion of inns and public houses, brewing had long been important – the town had three breweries until the closure of Crowleys in 1929. Nalder & Collyer's survived until 1936 and Page & Overton's until 1954. Tanning, milling, linen and calico bleaching (these three in close proximity to the parish church), chalk quarrying, lime burning and brick and tile making also gave employment. There were many gravel pits in north Croydon – the local path gravel being famous. A principal supplier was Hall & Company which had started at Merstham in 1824 and moved to Croydon in 1842. They became the largest coal merchants and sellers of building materials in the south of England but in the 1960s amalgamated with the Ham River Company and later became part of the Ready Mixed Concrete Company.

Carriage building became important, possibly because of the town's position on the busy Brighton Road. Certainly the firm of Lenny & Company in North End at one time employed more than 200 staff and exported carriages to Europe, but William Waters and Company of George Street claimed to be 'The Original Croydon Basket Carriage Manufactory'. Both firms were in the town during the 1820s and survived until around 1880. Iron, boots and shoes, fireworks, mineral water and ginger beer, clocks and bells, were amongst other local products and there were numerous laundries, printing works, building contractors and coal merchants. Croydon was for a time the film capital of Britain with several studios producing films in the early years of the 20th century, Clarendon, and Cricks & Martin being the best known. The gas-works moved from Surrey Street to Brimstone Barn at Waddon in 1877, and by 1891 the Corporation had established an electricity generating works at Pitlake.

As the 20th century progressed and the industries associated with agriculture declined, so light engineering started to expand. The opening of Purley Way as a bypass, and to serve the re-sited airport, led to many new factories being built to the west of the town.

By the late 1930s, the Croydon Foundry, the Standard Steel Company, Metal Propellors, Trojans (motor cars and vans), Waterman's Dyeing and Cleaning Works, Rollason Aviation Company, and Redwings, amongst others, were names of note. Other products included bedding and furniture, chocolate and confectionery, paints, radio sets, soap and perfumery. But there still remained a large number of small factories and workshops scattered around the town. All gave local employment and added variety to the townscape.

76. Domesday Book records a mill at Waddon. Following considerable enlargement in the 19th century it was, by 1924, one of only four mills still working on the River Wandle. In 1928 it was grinding 100 tons of wheat daily but it ceased work in that year. This view is dated *c*.1907.

77. A post mill was built at Shirley around 1809, but was destroyed by fire in 1854. The windmill shown here *c.*1950 replaced it shortly afterwards, and worked until the late 1890s. It is the last surviving windmill in Croydon, but at various times others existed at Westow Hill (Upper Norwood), Broad Green, Croydon Common (three briefly in the 1850s), and Coulsdon (two).

78. In the early 20th century farming was still carried on extensively in the locality. This postcard view of hay being loaded on to a cart at Park Hill *c.*1908 illustrates rural activity in close proximity to new houses, barely half a mile from the Town Hall. The house on the right was The Croft in Brownlow Road. The photographer was standing in a field on the corner of Brownlow and Selborne Roads.

79. A single row seed drill in use on rather infertile-looking land at Thornton Road, Thornton Heath, c.1911. In the background are several new houses at the end of Aurelia Road, and the chapel of Mitcham Road Cemetery. The chimneys are those of John Jakson & Company's Mitcham Road lavender water distillery.

80. The East Surrey Agricultural Association was based in the town and held regular meetings and events in the second half of the 19th century. The Croydon Farmers' Club was another local body concerned with agriculture.

EAST

AGRICULTURAL

SURREY

ASSOCIATION.

PLOUGHING MATCH.
THE DINNER
AT THE KING'S ARMS INN, CROYDON,
On WEDNESDAY, SEPTEMBER 25TH, 1861,

SAMUEL GURNEY, ESQ., M.P.
PRESIDENT FOR THE YEAR, IN THE CHAIR.

Dinner at Half-past 4 o'Clock. Tickets, 7s. each, including a pint of wine and dessert.

HENRY RICHARDS, *Hon. Sec.*

81.   A large cattle fair took place annually in October. At first it was held at Stubb's Mead, Pitlake, but it moved to Addiscombe Road and then to a field on the south side of Coombe Road. Finally it was held in a field on the west side of Brighton Road, on the edge of Haling Down near the *Windsor Castle*. This photograph shows the last fair on 2 October 1894. Croham Hurst is in the background and the steam from a passing train is visible. The *Purley Arms* is on the left, with houses on the east side of Brighton Road. A splendid display of agricultural implements is in evidence and there is a great deal of activity. Churchill Road now occupies the site.

82.   Long important in the meat trade, Croydon gained a purpose-built cattle market at Selsdon Road in 1848. Drovers Road marks the site and is a reminder that cattle and sheep were driven on foot for many miles to market, especially in the days before the railway came. It is recorded that in the 1860s Croydon Market could deal with 1,300 sheep, 200 calves and 300 pigs every week. This photograph dates from 1909. The market closed in 1935, and the *Surrey Drovers* public house in the background also closed several years later.

83. F. Stephen's East Surrey Monumental and Steam Masonry Works was in Brighton Road between Bartlett Street and Drovers Road. The sign in this photograph from the late 1890s claims it was 'the oldest business in Croydon'. This statement was incorrect as there were several much longer-established firms at that time. The firm last appeared in the local directory for 1910.

84. William Bell's smithy at Woodside was the last building in the village on the north side of the street just before the green and near the site later occupied by the war memorial. William Bell was the farrier from about 1880 until 1937 and this picture was taken in 1894. Smithies were very numerous in the Victorian and Edwardian periods, but gradually declined in importance and numbers as the 20th century progressed and the number of horses diminished.

85. Roffey & Clark took over the premises of F. Warren at 131 High Street around 1882, and when that (west) side of the street was cleared as part of the improvement scheme, the firm moved to a site between Grant's and the post office, where they remained until the 1970s. This postcard view shows the composing room of their printing works in Middle Street.

86. William E. Wilson opened a 'Tea Warehouse' at North End in about 1883 and by 1895 added an 'Oriental Cafe'. The restaurant became a favourite meeting place and the firm became famous in the district for their coffee, teas and bakery, and eventually had branches in Purley, Bromley and Sutton. This postcard view shows the tea blending, cutting and equalising machinery in use at 7 North End. Wilson's moved from North End to George Street c.1960 when their building was demolished for road widening. They were later taken over by Grant's and ceased trading in the late 1970s.

87. The Whitehorse Bakery of W. King was at 68 Whitehorse Road on the corner of Johnson Road, from 1911. Typical of the many corner shops that appeared all over the town, it provided local employment for a number of people as demonstrated here by the fine array of delivery vehicles, staff and family soon after it opened.

88. The Still family has been in the Croydon area for many years, farming at Chelsham, Addington and Shirley. This photograph shows a handcart used for milk deliveries in about 1906. The ladles were used to transfer milk into cans for delivery – not a very hygienic method.

89. The Holland Bottled Ales Stores of C. W. Willis was at 96 Sumner Road on the corner of Hatton Road, where this picture was taken *c.*1909. The van advertises Page & Overton's Celebrated Ales and Stout in casks of four-dozen, and bottles. Page & Overton's had public houses over much of west Kent, east Surrey and Sussex. The firm was taken over by Charringtons and the brewery eventually closed in 1954. The shop still exists as the Holland Stores.

90. By the 1860s Croydon had two rival fire brigades – the Croydon Volunteer Fire Brigade, depending entirely on voluntary subscriptions, and the Volunteer Fire Brigade, run by the Local Board of Health. The brigades merged in 1869 and the fire service was under corporation control for most of the period between 1883 until 1965, when it became part of the London Fire Brigade. Here men of the brigade are seen with Chief Officer John Dane (centre), a budding young fireman and the fire station cat c.1910.

91. The firm of Gillett & Johnston was founded by William Gillett who began work as a clockmaker at Hadlow in Kent,
moved to Clerkenwell, and then in 1844 to Croydon where he was joined by Charles Bland. The firm became known as
Gillett & Bland but in 1877 Arthur Johnston became a partner, the name was changed, and bells were added to its
products. By the early 20th century it was becoming world famous.
    On Tuesday 12 May 1925, King George V and Queen Mary made a private visit to the foundry at Union Road, off
Whitehorse Road, to inspect the 'greatest and most complete carillon of bells in the world'. This was the 53-bell carillon
weighing over 100 tons and constructed for the Park Avenue Baptist church in New York. The King and Queen arrived
by motor car at 3.00 p.m. and although it was a private visit, parts of London and St James's Roads were thronged and
some 2,000 to 3,000 people waited to greet them. That evening, crowds gathered in the vicinity of the foundry to hear
Monsieur Lefevre, from Belgium, give a recital on the carillon.

92. National Aircraft Factory No. 1 was erected on 240 acres of land south of Stafford Road and west of Coldharbour Lane, and included a flying testing ground, later to be known as Waddon Aerodrome. Building work started in September 1917 and production started in January 1918. This postcard view shows the fuselage and jig-making shop. With the arrival of peace in November 1918, the manufacturing of aircraft came to an end. In 1920 the factory was sold to Handley Page's Aircraft Disposal Company. Parts of the buildings are still in use for industrial purposes.

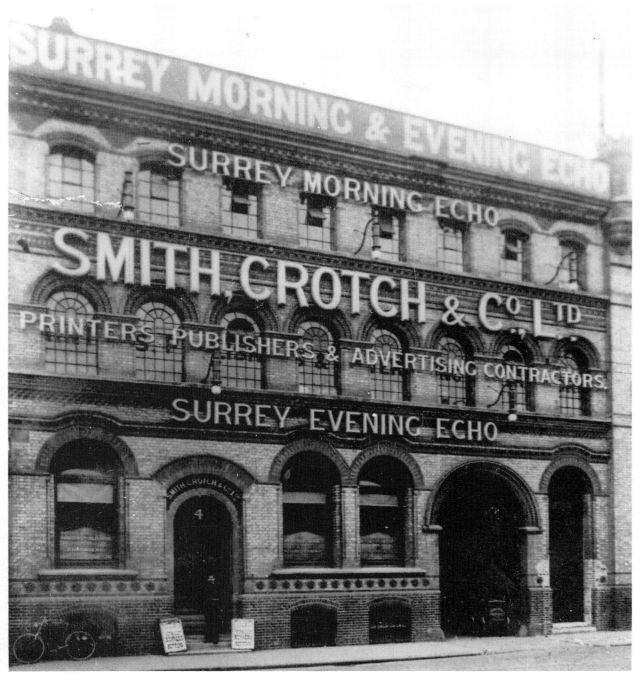

93. In common with most large towns, Croydon has had many local newspapers from the mid-19th century. The first to be published regularly was the *Croydon Chronicle*, started by Frederick Baldiston in 1855. Several attempts were made to publish daily papers, but probably due to the town's close proximity to London, these did not survive for very long. In 1905, the *Surrey Daily Argus* was launched. When this failed, the *Surrey Daily Echo* started as a morning and evening paper, in 1908, but only lasted a short while. The office and printing works seen here were for some years earlier, and from 1910, used by Ebbutt's as a furniture depository, but the building had from 1860 until 1894 housed John Cooper's Steam Boot Factory. Unusually for the shoe trade in the south of England, Cooper also employed outworkers and built 38 houses and several workshops in Bynes Road, near the *Red Deer*, to house them. Although listed, the building was demolished and the site redeveloped in the 1980s.

Transport

By 1851 the town centre was already served by two railway stations, with trains to London, Epsom, Brighton, Dover and intermediate places. Further railway expansion in 1855 saw the opening of a line to Wimbledon, followed by that along the Caterham Valley in 1856. Fierce competition between the Brighton and South Eastern railway companies resulted in the latter extending its Mid-Kent line to a terminus at Lower Addiscombe Road in 1864. Several other lines and stations opened at various times up to the end of the century and most of these stimulated house building in the immediate vicinity, for example at Selhurst and Thornton Heath. Through trains of the London & North Western Railway (for Willesden Junction) and the Great Eastern Railway (for Liverpool Street) served the town for many years.

Roads generally had poor surfaces, being very dusty and uneven. The local toll gates at Foxley Hatch (Purley), Long Lane (Woodside) and the *Swan and Sugar Loaf* were abolished in the 1860s. In 1879 the Croydon Tramways Company began operating horse-drawn trams from Surrey Street to the *Red Deer*, and from Crown Hill to Thornton Heath. The High Street was too narrow for the lines to be joined. Other routes were opened over the next few years. Some improvement to road surfaces along the routes resulted because tramway companies had to pave the roadway between the rails and for 18 inches on either side. As a consequence of the trams, parts of the town got their first regular local transport, making it possible for those who could afford the fares to live in more attractive or rural parts of the town, further from their place of work or the railway stations.

Motor vehicles started appearing on the streets towards the end of the century. In 1896 a 12 m.p.h. speed limit was introduced nationally and cars no longer had to be preceded by a man with a red flag. This event was celebrated by a run through the town to Brighton, which is commemorated each year on the first Sunday in November.

Reconstruction, electrification and extensions to the tramways came from 1901 with routes between Norbury and Purley, to Addiscombe, Penge, Crystal Palace, Thornton Heath, Sutton, Mitcham and Tooting. Some of these routes were built by the South Metropolitan Electric Tramways & Lighting Company, the rest by Croydon Corporation. Pleasure trips to the country on the open-top trams proved extremely popular in the early days. As the nearby country was built over, and the motor bus became more reliable, new bus routes encouraged people to take longer trips into Surrey, Sussex and Kent, far beyond the tram termini. Later a network of charabanc and motor coach services started, partly competing with the railways.

The Corporation had abandoned its Whitehorse Road and Addiscombe tram routes by 1926, and in 1933 all local buses and trams came under the control of the newly formed London Passenger Transport Board. This began to replace the local trams with trolley-buses between 1935 and 1937, leaving only the main tram route between Purley and London, and the branch to Thornton Heath, to survive the Second World War.

Road surfaces improved greatly from the early years of the 20th century and the 1920s and 1930s saw motor vehicles gradually supplant the horse for carrying goods. By the late 1930s horses remained in use mainly by milkmen, bakers, greengrocers and a few coal merchants, and in places such as the Ham Farm estate at Monks Orchard where heavy lorries frequently got bogged down in the unmetalled trackways. Numerous road improvements and widening schemes were adopted in the town centre and in the new suburbs and what was regarded as an *avant garde* bypass – Purley Way – was opened in 1924. Its purpose was to relieve traffic in the town centre and serve the aerodrome.

In 1920 Croydon Airport became the customs airport for London and remained so until the Second World War, when it was used as an R.A.F. fighter base. The scene of many of the great flights in the historical development of aviation, it put Croydon on the world map and its presence secured a large tract of open land which otherwise would no doubt have succumbed to the builder.

94. A train of the London, Brighton & South Coast Railway heads for Victoria, past farmland between Thornton Heath and Norbury on a sunny summer afternoon shortly before the First World War. The railway line between Balham and Selhurst was opened in 1862 and additional tracks were added in 1900. Housing development generally took place rather later along this line than along the line from Croydon to London Bridge, partly because of the larger number of people employed in the City compared with the West End, especially before the First World War.

95.   The railways provided much employment and even a small station usually had several members of staff to deal not only with passengers, but also with parcels and small items of freight, in the days when railways were common carriers. Here the staff at Thornton Heath pose on the platform *c.*1910.

96.   The London, Brighton & South Coast Railway suffered intense competition in the inner London area from 1903 because of the new electric tramways. In 1909, the company electrified its South London Line, using overhead current collection. In 1912 similar trains started running between Victoria and Selhurst via Crystal Palace from the new Selhurst depot. In 1925 the overhead electric services were extended through Croydon but only ran until 1929 because the newly created Southern Railway had decided to standardise on third rail current collection. Here an overhead electric train is approaching Windmill Bridge junction, just north of East Croydon.

97.   Most local lines were electrified on the third rail principle between 1926 and 1932. This typical scene shows the 12.02 p.m. Victoria to Coulsdon North train approaching East Croydon on 30 April 1950. The train dates from 1926, having been converted from even older rolling stock. The large water tower on the left provided the water supply for steam locomotives until the 1960s.

98.   Once the railways had become established, stagecoaches began to suffer from the competition and services gradually ceased. There was, however, a continuing interest in special trips. Here a stagecoach stands outside the *Hare & Hounds* public house at Waddon. The occasion and date are not recorded but it is thought to be some time in the Edwardian period.

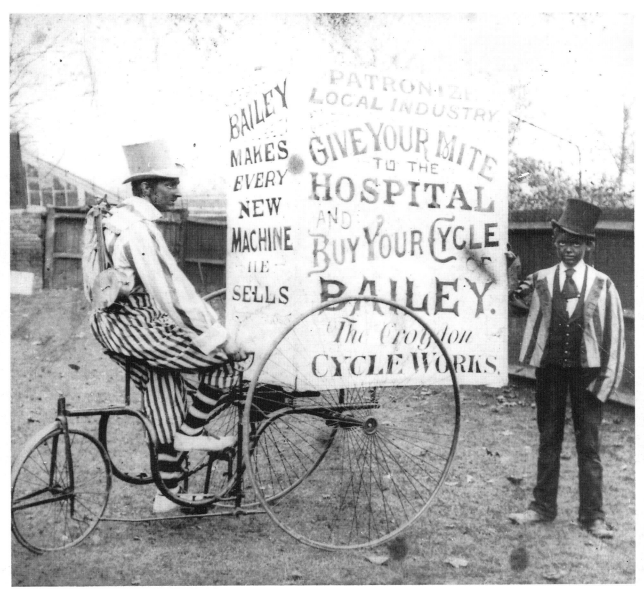

99.   The 'ordinary' or 'penny-farthing' cycle became popular by the 1880s, and the safety cycle emerged in very much its present form by the 1890s when there was a great craze for the activity. H. Bailey, cycle maker, was at 70A North End from *c*.1890 until *c*.1904. This photograph of a tricycle appears to date from the early 1890s and depicts a scheme both for advertising the firm and fund-raising for the hospital. It was quite acceptable at that time for men to appear disguised as negroes, and minstrel troupes were a popular form of entertainment.

100. Between 18 and 26 September 1903, the Automobile Club of Great Britain and Ireland arranged a 'Thousand Mile Trial'. Participants started at the Crystal Palace and on consecutive days (except Sunday) drove to Margate, Eastbourne, Worthing, Folkestone, Southsea, Bexhill, Winchester and Brighton. Here two of the entrants are travelling along Wellesley Road, approaching George Street, on one of the coastal runs. The underpass is now on the site where the men are carrying out roadworks.

101. The Croydon Central Motor Company's works was at 110 High Street, near Laud Street, but only seems to have survived for a few years, between 1910 and 1913.

corner of the Croydon Central Motor Co's Works.

Ring up 170 Croydon.
Always Available
Telegrams: Speed.

102. Numerous local laundries provided a useful service and considerable employment from the Edwardian period until the 1960s. There were more than 60 in the town in 1937. The entrance to the Whitehorse Sanitary Laundry was between 359 and 361 Whitehorse Road. This smart motor van of *c.*1909 illustrates the way in which the design of horse-drawn vehicle bodies was adapted for early motor vehicles. Stagecoach body design had been used similarly for the first railway carriages.

103. George T. Hall's coal and building material merchant's premises were at 132 George Street from the early 1880s until the 1950s. Steam lorries came into quite common use for heavy haulage purposes by the First World War and were not completely displaced until larger and more reliable motor lorries were available after the Second World War. This one was built by William Allchin of Northampton.

104. The local tramways were extended and electrified between 1901 and 1906. Brigstock Villa, right, housed the offices of the Croydon Corporation Tramways. Adjacent was the main tram depot and the single-deck works tram is standing just inside the entrance. A Corporation tram is turning into Brigstock Road from London Road on its way to Thornton Heath. An intrepid youth is hanging onto the back of the wagonette which is probably taking the occupants for a day in the countryside to the south of the town.

105. In the mid-19th century, the *Red Deer* had tea gardens and extensive stabling. The building seen here in 1922 was erected *c*.1900 by Alfred Bullock, a well-known local builder and contractor. The exterior has changed very little. Some of Thomas Tilling's motor buses are standing on the forecourt, which was used as a bus terminus for many years until about 1950. A driver is filling his radiator with water and the 12A bus on the right is just starting its journey to Oxford Circus.

106. As motor vehicles became more reliable, motor coaches began to replace wagonettes and brakes for outings. At first these early coaches, usually called charabancs, had canvas tops which could be pulled up over the vehicle to provide cover during inclement weather. This postcard view shows a staff outing using such vehicles, during the 1920s. The Croydon Co-operative Society had in 1914 merged with the Bromley, Beckenham and Penge Co-operative Societies to form the South Suburban Co-operative Society with its Head Office at 99 London Road, Croydon, where this picture was taken.

107. Trolleybuses were developed to use electric power but avoid the need for a fixed track set in the street. First introduced in the London area in 1931, they were seen as an efficient means of replacing trams, having the advantage of being able to stop by the kerbside instead of in the middle of the road. In the Croydon area, they replaced the trams on the Crystal Palace, Sutton and Mitcham routes between 1935 and 1937, but were themselves replaced by diesel buses in 1959 (Crystal Palace to Sutton) and 1960 (Croydon to Mitcham, etc.). Here a 654 trolleybus, dominated by the south tower of the Crystal Palace, descends Anerley Hill *c.*1938. This road was the former boundary between the parishes of Croydon and Penge but in the 16th century it had become so overgrown as to be impenetrable and following a legal dispute the boundary was moved further to the west.

108.   After the First World War it was decided to use the wartime airfields at Beddington and Waddon as the civil and customs airport for London. On 29 March 1920 the combined fields opened as Croydon Aerodrome. The original terminal building and control tower are seen here in the early 1920s. The airport at that time could hardly be termed glamorous and it has been described as 'resembling a wild-west township of the early mining days'.

109.   As civil aviation developed, better facilities were needed at Croydon. In 1928 new terminal buildings and a hotel were inaugurated on the recently opened Purley Way, which served as the Croydon bypass. Here one of the famous Handley Page HP 42 biplanes, *Horatius*, partially obscures the new control tower. The HP 42s were introduced in 1931 and gave reliable and safe service until the Second World War. After use by the R.A.F. between 1939 and 1945, the airport reverted to civil use until closure in 1959. The airport was by then considered too small for the larger planes coming into use.

VICARS-VIMY "CITY OF LONDON" UNLOADING LUGGAGE AT CROYDON.

110.   This Vickers Vimy plane, *City of London*, owned by Instone Airlines, commenced flying from Croydon in 1920. It had ten seats. The fare to Paris was £6 6s. single and £12 return. In 1924 Instone Airlines and other companies combined to form Imperial Airways, the forerunner of British Airways.

111. In the 1920s great hope was expressed for the future of airships and in 1921 the R33 airship took part in trials. A 140 ft. (43 m.) wooden mooring mast was built at Croydon as part of the experiment. The R33 arrived in July and the 600 ft. (182 m.) airship caused quite a stir on arrival, particularly because it dropped water ballast on the large crowd assembled to see it. The experiment was successful but the mooring mast had by mistake been built on private land, and had to be demolished.

112. Alan Cobham, probably the most famous British airman of his day, flew to Cape Town and back in 1925-6. It took him five months, flying from airfield to airfield around the world. This photograph shows his small aircraft, just to the right of the large Handley Page W 8, and also part of the huge crowd that greeted him on his return to Croydon on 13 March 1926. It is difficult now to appreciate the great interest and enthusiasm generated by the early flights and fliers. At the end of Lindbergh's flight across the Atlantic, it was estimated that 100,000 people were waiting at Croydon for his arrival.

Leisure and the Passing Scene

Between 1851 and the Second World War opportunities for leisure and social activities increased and altered dramatically. In the mid-Victorian period these depended greatly on one's class and sex; and in the absence of mass-media before the 1920s, local and national events created a great deal of interest and attracted vast crowds.

Hours of work were long, especially for those engaged in agriculture and service industries, conditions were hard, and for many incomes were low, so that most people had to create their own amusements and obtain pleasure from simple things. Family gatherings around the piano proved popular with the middle classes. But many poorer people spent much more than they could afford in public houses, though the churches and chapels and also various philanthropically-minded individuals formed clubs and associations where men could be amused, entertained, instructed and educated in less alcoholic surroundings. Some of these were highly popular and the wide range of membership fees indicates that some were specifically promoted to attract working men whilst others were designed to exclude them.

As in so many towns, the railway brought to the local fair (then still held on the Fairfield) a disorderly element which, in due course, led to riots; to its transfer to Pitlake on the Mitcham Road edge of the town; and, finally, to its abolition.

Horse racing had taken place locally since at least the 16th century. The racecourse at Woodside was opened in the 1860s and occupied an increasingly important place in the steeple-chasing world. In the 1880s opposition from local residents, most of whom had moved there after the racecourse had been established, led to closure in 1890. It was claimed that vast numbers of disorderly people were attracted and school attendances suffered. Sundays and Bank Holidays brought many visitors to Croydon as Londoners flocked to Shirley, Riddlesdown, Smitham Bottom and other favoured resorts in the neighbourhood. Again drunkenness and rowdyism was rife. The *Sandrock* public house at Shirley was particularly notorious until it lost its Sunday licence, following complaints about visitors dancing and singing in the road, courting more than one lady at a time, wearing false noses, exchanging head gear with those of the opposite sex, chaffing passers-by and bringing home branches of trees.

There were various local horticultural societies and also sport such as cricket which occupied many men with teams from such diverse bodies as the Early Closing Association, Croydon Gas Company, Messrs. Roffey & Clark (the printers and stationers) and even the Croydon Pawnbrokers.

Performances took place in the several theatres, although some people still regarded attendance at the theatre as being well on the way to damnation. Amateur dramatics later became popular under organisations such as the Croydon Players, Croydon Histrionic Society, Croydon Stagers Operatic and Dramatic Society, and Croydon Operatic and Dramatic Association.

Music, too, attracted a following with brass bands, choirs and orchestral groups. Names such as the Croydon Cecilia Society, the Croydon Church Choirs Union, the Excelsior Musical Society and the String Players Club no longer appear on local hoardings but Croydon Philharmonic Society has over 75 years of performances to its credit and there are others with a long history.

The cinema grew from providing modest performances in dangerously-converted shops to being a major attraction in the 1920s and 1930s with large and exotic super cinemas in many districts. The town has had some 35 cinemas at one time or another but only two remain.

113. Croydon was in good hunting country. Meets regularly started in the town centre, until the mid-19th century. The Victorian novelist, R. S. Surtees, vividly describes the local scene in *Jorrocks' Jaunts and Jollities*. This view of a meet of the Old Surrey Hounds outside the *Cricketers* at Addington dates from *c*.1910. The old parish church of St Mary's is in the background; five archbishops of Canterbury were buried there during the 19th century.

The Croydon Literary and Scientific Institution, founded in 1838, survived until 1929, and as lessee of the Public Halls provided a wide range of music, entertainment and educational activities. The Croydon Microscopical Club (later renamed the Croydon Natural History and Scientific Society), formed in 1870 and still flourishing, had its rooms and held soirées at these premises for many years. The Croydon Camera Club is another long-established body. It celebrated its centenary in 1990.

As the area developed so the growing need for public open spaces had to be met. Several of the town's open spaces such as Woodside Green, Croham Hurst, Addington Hills and Duppas Hill had long been used by the inhabitants for recreation although they were not in public ownership. In 1865 the Local Board of Health purchased Duppas Hill, the first of many open spaces to be obtained for permanent public use. A number of these were the subject of vigorous campaigns which prevented them being built over.

4. *Croydon Literary and Scientific*

INSTITUTION.

M

- -

MEMBER'S TICKET

FOR THE QUARTER ENDING SEPT. 30, 1863.

On Friday, July 31st, the

SUMMER FÊTE

WILL TAKE PLACE IN PART OF

The Grounds of R. Hutchinson, Esq., Park Lane,

Liberally placed at the service of the Committee for the occasion.

THE FULL
BAND OF THE HON. ARTILLERY COMPANY,
In Uniform—under the direction of Mr. Hird.

MR. LEVY (of the Crystal Palace,) will perform
SOLOS on the CORNET.

MR. E. W. MACKNEY, the celebrated Delineator of
Negro Character, is engaged.

The BAND of the Second Surrey Rifle Volunteers
Will perform at the close of the evening.

TO CONCLUDE WITH A

GRAND DISPLAY OF FIREWORKS

By MR. SOUTHBY, Pyrotechnist to the Queen.

☞ *The Grounds will be thrown open at* half-past FIVE *o'clock,
and the Band will commence very shortly after.*

REFRESHMENTS at Moderate Charges.

NOTICE.—This card entitles to the usual privileges of Membership, and, upon being produced, will admit to the Fête.

The Library will be closed on the day of the Fête.

2s. F. WARREN, Hon. Sec.

This Card admits the Lady Member only.

114. The Croydon Literary and Scientific Institution was established in 1838 at the instigation of Edward Westall, a surgeon. The Earl of Eldon, who lived at Shirley, was president. Originally intended as a mechanics' institute, its objects were stated as 'the diffusion of useful knowledge and by the careful exclusion from its proceedings of everything calculated to extend improperly the distinction of classes of sects, to promote among the inhabitants of the town and neighbourhood that harmony and good feeling that ought to exist among all men'. Classes and meetings were held in the Town Hall, later in the old theatre on Crown Hill, and then in the Public Halls in George Street. It was wound up in 1929.

THEATRE, CROYDON.

BY DESIRE, AND UNDER THE PATRONAGE OF THE

TRADESMEN OF CROYDON.

Mr. BARNETT has now the honour to announce a patronage kindly given for many years, with a prosperous result. It has happened that offence has been taken by parties who may not have been consulted on the occasion; when, however, the difficulty is considered of reaching each individual of so numerous a body, an excuse may easily be allowed, and all who are admirers of the drama, not only pardon the seeming neglect, but cheerfully unite in the general desire to have and to enjoy a pleasant and intellectual evening's amusement.

On WEDNESDAY, Nov. 12, 1834,

Will be acted the very highly celebrated Play, written by Mr. SHERIDAN KNOWLES, called The

HUNCHBACK.

Master Walter (the Hunchback), Mr. HARRINGTON.
Sir Thomas Clifford, Mr. BARRY.   Modus, Mr. MARSTON   Wilford, Mr. MORRIS.
Lord Tinsel, Mr. LACY.   Master Heartwell, Mr. BARNETT.
Fathom, Mr. WYATT.   Holdwell, Mr. CLAYTON.   Williams, Mr. PAICE.
Helen, Miss GORDON.   Julia, Mrs. BARNETT.

A FAVOURITE SONG, BY MRS. R. BARNETT.
A COMIC SONG, BY MR. WYATT.

The whole to conclude with the highly popular and greatly interesting and effective Melo-drama, called, The

WRECK
ASHORE;
OR, THE BRIDEGROOM FROM THE SEA.

PART I.—WINTER·
"Then came old January wrapt well
In many weeds to keep the cold away;
Yet did he quake and quiver like to quell,
And blow his nails to warm them if he may."—SPENSER.

Miles Bertram (Squire of Montley), Mr. HARRINGTON.   Captain Grampus (a Smuggler), Mr. BARRY.
Walter Barnard (a young farmer), Mr. MARSTON.
Marmaduke Magog (a Parish Constable), Mr. BARNETT.   Lieutenant of the Pressgang, Mr. MORRIS.
Andrew, Mr. PAICE.   William, Mr. CLAYTON.   Jemmy Starling (a Farmer's Boy), Mr. WYATT.
Alice, Mrs. BARNETT.   Bella (her sister), Mrs. R. BARNETT.   Dame Barnard, Mrs. RENAUD.

A lapse of five years is supposed to occur between each Part.

PART II.—SUMMER.
"And after her came jolly June arrayed
All in green leaves, as he a Player were."—SPENSER.

Miles Bertram (the Bridegroom and Captain of the Pirates), Mr. HARRINGTON.
Avery, Mr. MORRIS.   Grampus (an Outcast), Mr. BARRY.   Walter (a Sailor), Mr. MARSTON.
Marmaduke Magog (a Parish Beadle), Mr. BARNETT.   Jemmy Starling (a Married Man), Mr. WYATT.
Gaffer Fallowfield, Mr. PAICE.   Blackadder, Mr. CLAYTON.   Barbelot, Mr. LACY.
Alice (a Bridesmaid), Mrs. BARNETT.   Bella (the Bride), Mrs. R. BARNETT.
Mrs. Starling, Mrs. HARRINGTON.   Lucy, Miss ANDREWS.

Doors to be opened at Half-past Six o'Clock, and to begin at Seven precisely.
BOXES, 3s.—Half-price, 2s.   UPPER BOXES, 2s. 6d.—Half-price, 1s. 6d.   PIT, 2s.—Half-price, 1s.
GALLERY, 1s.—Half-price, 6d.   Half-price, at Half-past Eight o'Clock.
Tickets to be had of Mr. BARNETT, at Mr. Weller's, Watchmaker; and of Mr. ANNAN, Stationer, High Street, of whom Places for the Boxes may be taken

Nights of Performing will be, in future, Monday, Wednesday, Friday, and Saturday.

W. ANNAN PRINTER, CROYDON.

---

115. The earliest record of a theatre in the town is a poster advertising a performance in 1755 at the Widow Yeates's Large Theatrical Barn facing the Boarding School in Croydon. Around 1800 a theatre was erected in Crown Hill to replace an earlier one and in 1818 the Rev. D. W. Garrow wrote: 'Not many towns, perhaps, in the country, have a theatre exceeding this in neatness and convenience'. Edmund Kean and other famous celebrities played there. The building was later used by the Croydon Literary and Scientific Institution and the Theatre Royal was built on the site in 1873.

116.   The Grand Theatre and Opera House, pictured c.1905, was opened in 1896 by Herbert
Beerbohm Tree. It stood in the High Street adjacent to Wrencote (left) and opposite Whitgift Street.
In the same year the National Hall and Grand Theatre of Varieties (later the Empire) opened in the
former premises of the North End Circus. The Grand closed finally in 1959.

117. The Stanley Memorial Clock Tower in South Norwood was erected to mark the golden wedding of Mr. and Mrs.
Stanley and is seen here on the day of its inauguration, 29 June 1907. William Ford Stanley lived in South Norwood for
over 40 years. In 1901 he had built on the South Norwood Hill frontage of his estate, Cumberlow, a public hall and art
gallery, and later the Stanley Technical Trade School – a prototype secondary technical school. He was made a Freeman
of the Borough in 1907 and died in 1909.

118. The third Town Hall, designed by Charles Henman, junior, was opened on Tuesday 19 May 1896. Here the Hampshire Yeomanry are lined up in Katharine Street at 2.00 p.m. on that occasion. The Prince of Wales (later to be King Edward VII) had arrived by train with the Princess to perform the opening ceremony. The *Croydon Advertiser* reported that 'for hours after the departure of the royal visitors, the streets were crammed with people ... When darkness fell and the illuminations were fully displayed, the appearance of the town presented a brilliancy that Croydon has never surpassed'. Meanwhile vast crowds watched a display of fireworks in Wandle Park by Messrs. Brock & Co. of South Norwood.

Croydon Lifeboat Day

119. The town was crowded on Wednesday 22 July 1908 for the first Lifeboat Day Carnival for 10 years. Over 200 horses were involved in the two processions which included the Southend and Eastbourne lifeboats, and which toured much of the town. There were competitions for those in fancy dress, for decorated bicycles and motor cars, and prizes for those who collected the most money. Here part of one of the processions is in Cherry Orchard Road outside the postal sorting office. The grounds of Brickwood House on the left are being prepared for the construction of the new roller-skating rink.

120. Beckenham golf course, on the site of the former Croydon racecourse at Woodside, was the first in the area, and opened in 1893. Croham Hurst Golf Club was formed in 1911, and this postcard view shows the entrance at the corner of Croham and Croham Manor roads. This part of the course has for many years been used as playing fields by the Old Whitgiftian Association, whose members bought it from the Whitgift Foundation as a memorial to old boys killed in the Second World War.

121. The Brighton Road has seen a great variety of sporting events. Here some of the participants in a London to Brighton walk of 1904 are in London Road, near Broad Green. Note the proliferation of advertisements.

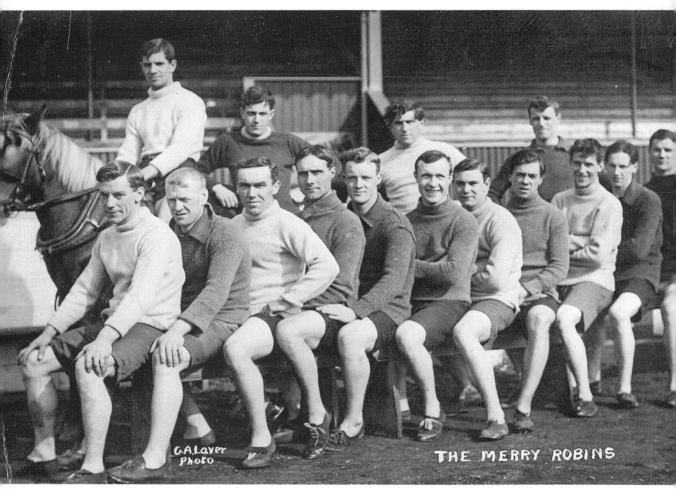

THE MERRY ROBINS

G.A.Loyer
Photo

122. Croydon Common Football Club developed from a team based at St Luke's Mission church at the junction of Boulogne and Princess Roads. As a professional team from 1907 and known as 'The Robins', it played at The Nest in Selhurst Road, now part of the site of Selhurst railway depot. The team ceased playing during the First World War and the ground was taken over by Crystal Palace F.C. until its move to Selhurst Park. In this photograph of the Croydon Common team in the 1913-14 season, Jack Little is seated on the horse. Standing from left to right are Thomas Newton, Arthur Hutchins and Billy Yenson. Seated from left to right are Percy Barnfather, Arthur Pace, Albert Chester, Billy Bushell, Percy Page, Dick Allison, – Pillinger, Dick Upex, Robert Nash, – Gowan and Ernest Williamson.

123 & 124. The popularity of particular pastimes often fluctuates over the years. An open air roller-skating rink occupied a site at Mint Walk between 1875 and 1892. In 1909 there was another short-lived craze for this activity when a roller-skating rink was built on the corner of Cherry Orchard and Addiscombe Roads. This postcard view appeared as a photograph in the *Croydon Chronicle* of 19 February 1910 under the heading 'Rinkomania in Croydon. The Pastime of the Moment'. In 1915, George Frederick Creed transferred his teleprinter business into the building, and the rink became the machine shop until closure of the works in 1966. The advertisement is also from a contemporary postcard.

THE SKATING RINK,
Cherry Orchard Road,
CROYDON.

DAILY:
10-30 a.m.
2-30 p.m.
7-0 p.m.

Popular Prices:
6d. including Hire of Skates.
Spectators, Admission 3d.

125 & 126.   Owned by the Pazzi family, the *Café Royal* in North End was a popular rendezvous for several generations of well-to-do Croydonians between 1896 and its closure in the 1950s. Weddings and other special functions were catered for as this advertising postcard from *c.*1905 indicates. The prices may appear very low by current standards but at that time an average weekly wage of 35s. was quite usual for a clerk with a wife and family to support.

127.   Dr. Malcolm Sargent conducting a concert by the London Philharmonic Orchestra at the North End Hall on Wednesday 30 March 1938. The hall, formerly the meeting place of the North End Brotherhood, was later purchased by the Corporation and renamed the Civic Hall. It was closed and demolished on the opening of the Fairfield Halls in 1962.

128.   Brass bands were extremely popular in the Edwardian period and many large commercial organisations and institutions had their own. Providing music for the pleasure of themselves and others, they often entered competitions and performed at local events and in the parks, a number of which had bandstands. The band of the Croydon District Postal Musical Society was photographed at the lower end of Farthing Downs, near Marlpit Lane, Coulsdon *c.*1908.

129.   The Town Hall Gardens were laid out in 1896 in the cutting formerly occupied by the railway tracks leading to the Central station. The gardens were at first only 'temporarily open upon such days and times as shall be settled by the Mayor' but by 1898 opening on Sundays and in the evenings was agreed. In the early 1980s the gardens were extended over the site of the former police station and part of Mint Walk. The enlarged area was opened and named the Queen's Gardens on the occasion of the visit by the Queen in 1983, in celebration of the centenary of the borough.

The World & its Wonders
Week by Week

Comedy

Continuous Performance

Farce:

Plays without Words

THE PICTURE
PLAYHOUSE.

ELECTRIC

PALACE.

THE RETREAT

130.   Many early cinemas were in converted shops or other buildings. Croydon's first was the Station Picture Hall in Station Road, West Croydon, opened in 1908. The Electric Palace in Thornton Heath was in the High Street on the corner of The Retreat. In this case the shop was converted into the entrance, and the auditorium, with 600 seats and space for 200 standing, was built behind. It closed in 1923, and by 1927 had been converted into the Palais de Danse.

131.   The first scout troop in the town was formed in May 1908 and nine were registered by the end of that year. By 1910 troops at Wallington, Carshalton, Burgh Heath, Banstead, Tadworth and Warlingham had all been registered as Croydon troops, but in 1912 Sutton District was formed to take some of these and later Coulsdon and Purley District was set up similarly.

The 26th Croydon (1st Coulsdon) troop was founded by Scoutmaster R. Nightingale in November 1914, and the wolf cubs of that troop are pictured here in a field by Coulsdon and Smitham Downs station c.1920. The station opened in 1899 with the name of Stoat's Nest, the same as that of one opened in 1841 a few hundred yards further north, but which had closed in 1856. Following a tragic railway accident in 1909 in which a number of people were killed and injured, and when the first to arrive at the scene with a stretcher were the Purley, Coulsdon and District Scout troop, the station was renamed Coulsdon and Smitham Downs, and then Coulsdon North in 1923. It closed finally in 1983.

132.   The breezy heights of Riddlesdown were purchased by the City of London Corporation in 1883. The popularity of the Downs was enhanced by the opening in 1893 of William Gardner's Pleasure Resort, Temperance Hotel and Tea Gardens. Attractions over the years included donkeys, a museum, monkey house, aviary, swings, hoop-la, coconut stalls, swing boats and a miniature railway. Its fame increased and by 1906 refreshments could be provided for over 2,000 people at a time. On August Bank Holiday 1908, more than 4,000 visitors were catered for. William Gardner died in 1930, and part of the site was sold for development. The house seen here survives as 23 Godstone Road.

133. Children frequently used the streets for games until the increase of motor traffic from the early 1950s. Here a group stand in Whytecliffe Road, Purley c.1905. Hoops were very popular before the Second World War.

134. Land at Frog's Mead and Stubb's Mead, Pitlake, was laid out by the Corporation as Wandle Park in 1890. With large areas of water, fed by the springs of the River Wandle, boating was popular. Another seasonal pursuit was skating, as photographed here on 5 December 1925. Neither of the people nearest to the camera appears confident of their ability to stay upright.

135.   Opened in 1935, Purley Way Swimming Pool was 200 ft. (60 m.) long and 70 ft. (21 m.) wide. It could hold 1,200 people and was very crowded on fine days. In the Second World War, being in a restricted area just opposite the airport, it was closed to the public but was used for air-sea rescue training purposes. Re-opened after the war, major repairs were needed by the 1970s, and it was closed in 1979.

136.   Croydon traders inaugurated the 'Streets of Adventure' carnival in 1927 to raise funds for Croydon General Hospital. It was held each year on a summer Wednesday afternoon (early closing day) until the outbreak of war in 1939. This view shows the carnival fair which was held at Wandle Park in 1937 or 1938.

Church, Chapel and School

During the Victorian period and well into the 20th century, religion played a most important part in everyday life. As in all growing towns the number of churches and chapels in Croydon increased in line with the town's expansion. Sunday worship was considered obligatory for many – certainly those belonging to the respectable upper and middle classes. Historically the Anglicans were the greatest force in the town although until 1829 the parish church of St John the Baptist was their only place of worship. As the Victorian development occurred, many Anglican churches were built in the newly growing districts – some in the evangelical tradition (e.g. Christ Church, Sumner Road), and some being strongholds of the Oxford movement (e.g. St John the Evangelist, Upper Norwood).

137. This 1860 photograph shows the old parish church of St John the Baptist from St John's (later renamed Rectory) Grove. The road surface is in a very poor state. This was quite usual in the Victorian period.

From the 16th century until the late 1830s there was no centre for Roman Catholic worship in the town. From 1837, within the first decade of Catholic emancipation, there was a Catholic chapel at 20 Southbridge Road, and this led, via a cottage at Broad Green, to the establishment of St Mary's church, Wellesley Road, in the 1860s.

A wide variety of other religious persuasions was catered for. The Society of Friends (Quakers) had strong local connections and non-conformists such as Baptists and Methodists spread their gospel and buildings around the town. Some of these congregations were well-to-do. West Croydon Baptist church (Spurgeon's Tabernacle) was particularly fashionable in Victorian times. Other non-conformist buildings such as the dignified Baptist chapel in Tamworth Road (1866) and the Providence Strict and Particular Baptist chapel in West Street (1847) were less flamboyant and doubtless attracted a more humble class of worshipper. Much good work was done amongst the poor by the wealthier members of the congregations of the churches, with the provision of money, clothing and food, or missionary work. The first Christian Mission outside the East End of London was established in Croydon by William Booth in 1869. This, in 1878, was renamed the Salvation Army. The Congregationalists, too, became a force in the town – two of their more prominent churches being now used by other religious bodies.

138. At about 10.45 p.m. on the night of 5 January 1867, a fire was discovered in the parish church. A snowstorm had started and the wind spread the flames. It was 35 minutes before water could be obtained and, apart from the tower, the building was gutted. Many fine memorials were destroyed, but those of Archbishops Whitgift and Sheldon have subsequently been restored. This painting by John Nash was commissioned to help raise funds for reconstruction. The new, slightly enlarged, church was consecrated in 1870.

139. As the population of the ancient parish of Croydon increased, so more churches were needed, and new parishes were formed. In 1829, those of All Saints', Upper Norwood and St James', Croydon Common were created. This view of the interior of St James' church dates c.1910.

140. The church of St Peter in South Croydon was designed by George Gilbert Scott, who later lived at nearby Blunt House. It was dedicated in 1851. The use of knapped flints as a facing material was very common locally for many types of building. The spire was added in 1864, and when almost complete was destroyed by fire and had to be rebuilt. This view is dated 1866.

141. Baptists of the Calvinistic Strict Communion Order had been active in the town and had a chapel there in 1726. A broader Baptist church was thought necessary, and following a meeting in 1868, with Joshua Allder prominent among those present, an iron church in Wellesley Road was purchased from the Presbyterians. Services started in 1869 and the foundation stone of the new building, seen here in about 1910, was laid in 1872. The Rev. James A. Spurgeon (brother of the famous Charles Haddon Spurgeon) was pastor from 1870 to 1899. The church is still known as Spurgeon's Tabernacle, and the adjacent railway bridge as Spurgeon's Bridge.

GEORGE ST. CHAPEL DORCAS SOCIETY

FOR THE INDUSTRIOUS POOR.

This Ticket will entitle _____
to purchase articles to the amount of *four shillings*, on payment of *two shillings*.

THE SALE

TO BE HELD IN

THE SCHOOL ROOM OF THE CHAPEL,

On _____

FROM HALF-PAST TEN TILL HALF-PAST TWELVE O'CLOCK.

Recommended by _____ *Subscriber.*

N.B.—This Ticket can only be used to purchase articles at the Sale for which dated.

142. The importance of churches, chapels and religion was immense in the Victorian and Edwardian periods and their good work for poorer people compensated to some extent for the lack of formal state care. George Street Chapel Dorcas Society had for its object 'the making up by ladies of the congregation of useful clothing'. The poor were allowed to purchase this at the cost price of the material, and on spending 2s. to have additional items to the value of 2s. free of charge.

143. The Gospel Temperance Hall opened in 1894, in Mint Walk opposite the rear of the Town Hall. It was built for the Croydon Blue Ribbon Gospel Temperance Union and was similar in style to a number of iron chapels around the town. The band was photographed outside the hall *c.*1908.

Schooling was not neglected and before the Croydon School Board was created in 1871 the town's schools were mainly in one of three categories: Anglican church schools such as Parish Church (1851); long established private foundations by Archbishops Whitgift (1599) and Tenison (1714); and small, independent schools which at one extreme took boy boarders, perhaps up to university entrance age and at the other were dame schools like one in a cottage in Cross Road. One prominent school falling outside these categories was the non-conformist British School which was open from 1812 until 1951.

The Croydon School Board (1871) and its successor Education Committee (1902) had the function of making education available in those growing parts of the town where provision was otherwise inadequate. The Anglican church meanwhile failed to invest sufficient money in its school buildings to enable some of them to remain open, one of the earliest closures being St James's in 1909.

144. Looking east c.1830 along Addiscombe Road, now the eastern part of George Street. New Lane (later renamed Wellesley Road) is to the left and Park (formerly Back) Lane is to the right. On the right is Fairfield House School, later run by Alfred Twentyman until around 1875. According to one of his pupils, Mr. Twentyman 'had no recognised qualifications as a teacher except an enviable power to instil confidence in parents and to create deportment and a use of good manners in his boys, many of whom did well in after life'.

From 1902, also, the Local Education Authority could provide secondary education, the Borough (later Selhurst) Boys' and Girls' Grammar schools being opened in 1904 followed by Central schools such as Lady Edridge, John Ruskin, and Heath Clark. In the meantime the private sector had put its house in order. The Whitgift Foundation had evolved two schools, both for boys; and girls were able to gain entrance to Croydon High (from 1874), Old Palace (1887) and Croham Hurst (1899).

· Croydon College, now at Fairfield, has its origins in two separate institutions. These were Croydon School of Art, founded remarkably early, in 1868, and whose first principal was publicly sacked in front of his students; and the Pitlake Technical Institute, founded in 1888 by the Rev. J. Oakley Coles who became a curate at the parish church after practising for a while as a dentist. He taught at the Institute, and once told a member of the congregation, who suggested that woodcarving and clay modelling were unseemly subjects for a curate to teach, that there was at least one carpenter to whom the Church owed a great debt. The 1868 date attributable to the School of Art makes Croydon College one of the oldest Further Education institutions in the country.

145.   This interior view of St Andrew's school-house shows the parlour, with gas lighting, piano and the many ornaments usual in Victorian and Edwardian homes. The school-house was at the time the home of Miss Mary Large, Headmistress of the Infants school from 1882 until 1921.

146.   Archbishop John Whitgift laid the foundation stone of his hospital on 22 March 1596. This event is still commemorated when the brothers and sisters of the hospital and boys of the Whitgift and Trinity schools attend an annual service at Croydon parish church to give thanks for the benefactions of their founder. From 1889 it became the custom for the boys to march through the town from their respective schools to the church, but when Trinity moved to Shirley in 1965 this feature was discontinued. Here the boys of the grammar school, all wearing white flowers, are entering the church on Founder's Day in 1913.

147.   The Friends' School moved from Islington to Croydon in 1825, using this impressive Georgian house and adding a large wing on either side. These wings were demolished after the school moved to Saffron Walden in 1879. The house, dating from 1708, later became a school again and was known as St Anselm's between about 1910 and 1940, when it was destroyed by a land mine. It stood in Park Lane, approximately where it is now joined by the flyover.

148. In 1714 Archbishop Tenison founded and endowed a perpetual charity school for 10 poor boys and also, unusually, 10 poor girls which made it one of the first co-educational schools in the country. This was at North End but in 1852 it moved to a site near the new St Peter's church. In 1959 it again moved, this time to Selborne Road. This photograph shows girls of class III *c*.1900. Note the flint walls of the building.

149. Catholic schools were provided locally from the early 1860s, and later there was a particularly strong Catholic connection in the Upper Norwood area. St Joseph's College moved to Beulah Hill in 1903 having previously occupied several sites in south London. This view shows a woodwork class in the 1930s.

150. Pupils and staff of St John's Church School, Bradmore Green, Coulsdon, photographed on 25 July 1930, with the 'Junior Shield', in front of the school-house. Miss Ada Churchill, the headmistress (thought to be the woman on the right) lived there from 1912 until her retirement in 1932. The school at this time was the second to occupy the site, and was in use from 1886 to 1963. It was once recorded that nearby was an osier bed 'where canes were cut to punish the fractious'.

151. Children of Addington Village School photographed in an adjacent field c.1907. The school may have opened as early as 1844 and pupils came from a large rural area, many having to walk long distances. At one time the vicar suggested the introduction of earlier school sessions so that children could help with the harvest and other rural activities. During the shooting season boys were regularly employed by farmers and the gentlemen of the district to bag game, carry cartridges, or act as beaters, to the concern of the Master who was unable to enter them for the annual examination if they failed to make the requisite number of attendances. Entries in the school log books record many absences due to such practices even up to the years just before the First World War. The last virtually unaltered village school in Croydon, it closed in 1950.

152. Drill was important at most schools in the late Victorian and Edwardian periods. The Asylum for Fatherless Children (renamed Reedham Orphanage in 1904) was established at Purley for 300 boys and girls by Dr. Andrew Reed, a congregational minister, in 1858. The school attached to the orphanage claimed that 'Reedham Drill' was known world-wide, and here scholars are seen performing it *c.*1906. By 1950 numbers had fallen away and the school was opened up to local children. The orphanage was demolished in 1980.

Some Croydon Personalities

Croydon has at various times had a number of well-known residents including Arthur Conan Doyle, Camille Pisarro, Emile Zola, Samuel Coleridge Taylor, David Herbert Lawrence, Malcolm Muggeridge and Basil Dean, to mention just a few. But in common with most large places many people have contributed a great deal to the life of the town, to its growth and to its cultural and general well-being.

Croydon was fortunate that during its rapid development between 1851 and the 1930s a number of public spirited people with progressive ideas settled in the town. Their names are now almost forgotten but men such as Cuthbert Johnson, Jesse Ward and a host of others ought to be remembered. A few of them are represented here and most are men, which is perhaps a reflection of the period. The contribution of women should not be forgotten, or that of the countless numbers who have devoted much of their time and effort over the years to local voluntary organisations which have done so much for the good of the town and its residents.

153. Born in 1825, Dr. Alfred Carpenter became well-known both locally and nationally as a pioneer in sanitary science. He was a member of the Local Board of Health for many years, a leading figure in the revival of the Literary and Scientific Institution and was second president of the Croydon Microscopical Club. More than any other single person he was responsible for the creation of Croydon General Hospital. He was medical officer to four successive archbishops and died in 1892.

154. Born in 1846, the Rev. John Masterman Braithwaite came to Croydon as Vicar in 1882. Although he was in the town for less than seven years, his sudden and untimely death in 1889 was the subject of the first leader in the *Croydon Advertiser*. Over 500 official mourners attended his funeral, and hundreds of Croydonians lined the streets as his coffin passed on its way from the parish church to Queen's Road Cemetery. Prominent in the movement for free public libraries, his memory is perpetuated as the reference library in the new Town Hall was named Braithwaite Hall. He left seven children, one of whom was to become the famous actress, Dame Lilian Braithwaite.

155. Baldwin Latham became surveyor at Ely in 1860. Three years later he was appointed Engineer and Surveyor to the Croydon Local Board of Health and was responsible for the development of Beddington Sewage Farm on the irrigation principle. He enlarged the local waterworks and built the water tower on Park Hill. In 1871 he became a consulting engineer and was responsible for designing waterworks on the continent, including Vienna. He resided at Park Hill House at the time of his death, at the age of 80, in 1917.

156. Henry Overton was born in 1791 at his father's house in Butcher Row. In 1814 he started Overton's Brewery and this was continued by his son, Frederick, after Henry's death in 1864. In 1892 it became Page & Overton's. In 1827, Messrs. Barnard and Defries established a gas-works nearby and in 1829 Henry Overton purchased it. In 1847 the Croydon Commercial Gas & Coke Company was formed to take over the works and Henry Overton became a director.

157. William Inkpen was born in 1789 and for many years operated stagecoaches between Croydon and London. His office was in the High Street where he also ran a saddlery business. He almost invariably drove one of his teams of horses and had a strong – not unnatural – antipathy towards railways on which he never once travelled. He was a member of the Improvement Commissioners for some time from 1829 and director of the Croydon Gas Company from 1847, and chairman from 1855-8. Inkpen was also a member of the Board of Guardians for 17 years and chairman for several of them. He was photographed with E. Ford, his constant companion for 26 years, a few years before he died at his home in George Street in 1873.

158. Born at Leith in 1843, Jabez Spencer Balfour was the most popular man in Croydon in the years up to 1892, after which he was the most reviled. When he first came to Croydon he lived at London Road, and later at Wellesley House which stood approximately where the Wellesley Road multi-storey car park is today. Taking an interest in practically every movement in the town, he was natural choice for Charter Mayor in 1883. He was at that time Liberal M.P. for Tamworth and later became M.P. for Burnley. As a young man he had shown a genius for speculation and became associated with a group of companies of which the Liberator Building Society was the principal one. In September 1892, this society failed and Balfour fled to South America. Eventually he was arrested there, extradited and sentenced to 14 years' hard labour. Many thousands of small savers had lost their life savings in the collapse of the various companies with which Balfour was involved. He died in 1916.

159. On 20 March 1918 Croydon Education Committee closed the schools for the afternoon so that teachers could join in Women's Citizens' Day, celebrating franchise reform. Many Croydonians had been active in the suffrage movement and following a service at the parish church conducted by the Vicar, Canon White-Thompson, a procession of women marched along Old Town, Whitgift Street and High Street led by the Mayoress, Mrs. Houlder, Mrs. Henry Fawcett ('Mother' of the women's suffrage movement) and Miss Nina Boyle. Here the Mayoress is presenting an address to the Mayor, Alderman Howard Houlder, on the Town Hall steps. Alongside is the Town Clerk, Dr. John Newnham. The Mayor gave a suitable response and then marched with the women to the Public Hall where there were speeches.

Alderman Houlder was mayor in four successive years and both he and his wife were made Freemen of the town in 1920. Four years later, the shipping company that he owned went into liquidation on account of the economic slump. He became personally bankrupt and retired to Sussex.

160. On Tuesday 1 May 1894, the ceremony of beating the bounds of the parish took place. The *Croydon Advertiser* reported that 'the party met shortly before 10 o'clock at East Croydon station, and proceeded by train to Purley and then to a point at Foxley Hatch. The perambulation started from here and on reaching the boundary at Streatham adjourned to luncheon at the *King William IV* Hotel'. The party, photographed here when about to set off for Upper Norwood after lunch, included a number of local worthies. Charles Elborough, the Town Clerk (who died the following year) is on the right, Robert Ridge is second from right, Henry Seale, Vestry Clerk, is in the centre and Alderman Miller is wearing a top hat. Boys of the Parish Church School and several other people whose names are not recorded were also present.

161. Dr. R. W. Wilson was appointed Medical Officer of the Croydon Union Infirmary at an annual salary of £200 when it opened in 1885. He also received £126 per annum as medical officer for the infectious wards at the workhouse plus 1s. 6d. for every vaccination and 10s. 6d. for each maternity delivery. He is pictured here at his retirement presentation on the lawn by the Woodcroft Road entrance of the infirmary (which is now Mayday Hospital), on 13 July 1922. He was presented with a chiming clock in a mahogany case as the parting gift of Croydon Union and with a china tea service from the patients. Those on the platform include Mr. N. P. Walker, Clerk to the Guardians, and Mr. W. H. Menear, Chairman of the Board.

162.   Edward A. Martin (left) was born in Brighton in 1864 and died there in 1943. Naturalist, geologist and author, he lived in Croydon for much of his life and was a member of the Borough Library Committee from 1902 until 1936, and vice-chairman from 1926 to 1936. He was also Curator of the Grange Wood Museum from 1901 until 1936. He is pictured here with Henry Keatley Moore in about 1900. Both were prominent in the campaigns to save Croham Hurst from building development and to prevent the demolition of the Whitgift Hospital.

Henry Keatley Moore was born in London in 1846 of a Surrey family and came to Croydon in 1868. His family was closely involved in the establishment of a Unitarian church in the town. He was active in founding the Croydon branch of the University Extension Movement and was a very good musician. Elected to the Town Council in 1893, he remained a member until 1932 when he was 86. He was Mayor in 1906-8 and was made a Freeman of the Borough in 1917. As a member, and Chairman (1902-12) of the Library Committee, he was largely responsible, with Louis Stanley Jast, Chief Librarian, for introducing open access and numerous other revolutionary ideas in public library practice which made Croydon libraries famous at that time. He died in 1937, aged 91.

163.   Peggy (later Dame Peggy) Ashcroft (left) was born in 1907 at Tirlemont Road, South Croydon. She attended Woodford School and soon became famous as an actress. The Ashcroft Theatre in Croydon is named after her. She is pictured here with the Mayor, Alderman Thomas Arthur Lewis and Brenda, his daughter, at the opening of the tenth annual Surrey Handicrafts Exhibition at the Public Halls on Tuesday 14 October 1930. Organised by the Surrey Garden Village Trust, a smallholders' co-operative organisation, the exhibition lasted several days and the *Croydon Advertiser* reported that it was well-attended with over 1,000 competition entries from as far afield as Huddersfield and Barrow-in-Furness. Alderman Lewis came to Upper Norwood in 1879 and claimed to be one of the town's pioneer motorists. He became a councillor in 1911 and was Mayor for two years from 1929. He died in 1941, aged 77.

The First World War

The effects of the war soon became apparent locally. Guards appeared at railway bridges, signal boxes, water reservoirs, gas and electricity works, and other important installations. Volunteers of the Croydon National Reserve selected and commandeered horses and vehicles from firms considered able to spare them. Train services were severely restricted. Huge notices appeared directing people 'To the Recruiting Office' with a large arrow pointing the way. Reduced street lighting and a degree of black-out was introduced.

One tram was converted into a mobile recruiting office and toured the town, while another carried a searchlight on the upper deck, to be used in detecting Zeppelins which might approach the area.

Belgian refugees soon arrived and were found accommodation locally. In 1915 a national 'no treating' order prevented anyone offering a friend intoxicating liquor on licensed premises. It was claimed this brought great sobriety and contributed to the significant decrease in crime.

All building development ceased and road maintenance suffered badly. Severe food shortages continued with rationing introduced, rather belatedly, in 1918.

But overshadowing everything was the constant anxious waiting for news of family and friends serving abroad. Some 25,000 Croydon men went to the war. Two thousand five hundred never returned, and 10,000 came back wounded.

164.   The Fourth Queen's Royal Regiment was Croydon's territorial battalion and had originated in the 1850s as the Croydon Rifle Volunteer Company. Photographed on 5 August 1914, the territorials have marched from Mitcham Road Barracks and are in London Road, passing Oakfield Road, on their way to East Croydon station where the foot soldiers embarked for Strood.

165.   Davidson Road, Ecclesbourne Road, Ingram Road and Stanford Road (later Norbury Manor) council schools, and the boys' and girls' secondary schools at The Crescent, were converted into war hospitals between 1915 and 1919. Over 1,000 beds were provided. The staff came from the RAMC, as seen here at Ecclesbourne Road on 3 April 1916. The NCOs' mess room apparently provided a good meal, liberally washed down with White's lemonade.

166.   Addington Palace, country home of the archbishops between 1809 and 1896, was converted into a war hospital. This postcard view sent on 3 September 1915 has the following message: 'This is the place I have moved to for six weeks. It is a very nice place, about five miles of ground to go about. These are old paitents [*sic*] on fire drill they learn that in case of fire in the palace.'

167.   On Wednesday 13 October 1915, a lone Zeppelin made a bombing run over Croydon. Eighteen high explosive bombs were dropped, demolishing houses in Edridge, Beech House, Chatsworth, Oval, Morland and Stretton Roads. Nine people were killed. This photograph shows damage in Edridge Road. In 1916, on 23 September, four high explosive bombs were dropped by a Zeppelin in the Downscourt Road and Hall Way area of Purley but did very little damage.

The Second World War

With the threat of war increasingly apparent in the mid-1930s, refugees began to arrive from the continent. National and local preparations were well advanced by the end of 1939 – much more than they had been in 1914. Gas masks had been issued, schoolchildren evacuated, a total black-out introduced at night, air raid shelters built and a national savings campaign started. A Home Guard was set up in 1940 and food rationing was introduced. Anti-aircraft guns and barrage balloons were placed at various sites around

168.   In January 1939 the government declared Croydon a neutral zone under their air raid precautions scheme. This meant no public evacuation from, or into, the area would be allowed in the event of war. The Corporation protested and Croydon was then designated an evacuation zone and plans were prepared. On Monday 4 September 1939 about 18,000 Croydon children, teachers and helpers were evacuated. All schoolchildren were labelled, and, carrying their gas masks and belongings, set out rather apprehensively, unsure what the future would bring. Here, some of the evacuees are making their way across George Street into East Croydon station.

the town – with Croydon, Biggin Hill and Kenley airfields nearby, Croydon seemed a likely target for enemy attack.

By June 1940 the Battle of Britain had started and the clear skies above the town were the scene of much conflict in the following months. Eight bombs fell on fields at Addington on 17 June 1940 in the first raid on the London area. Then on 15 August that year a group of German aircraft attacked Croydon Airport before any warning was given. Much damage occurred in the immediate area with 62 people killed, 37 seriously injured and 137 slightly injured. The particularly severe bombing during the Blitz between August and September 1940 and May 1941 saw many more bombs fall on Croydon with nearly 1,100 houses destroyed, some 26,000 damaged and 362 people killed. In 1944, the flying bomb (V1) attacks wreaked havoc. Nearly 3,000 workmen, including 1,500 from around the country, who had to be found local accommodation, were needed for repair work.

Many local people had the added worries over friends and family serving in the forces, and the Second World War also had a much greater impact on the civilian population than the first. It also served to halt the relentless outward spread of building which had threatened to engulf the nearby Surrey countryside and gave a breathing space for the Green Belt to become effective. That perhaps was the one local good, lasting result.

169. Preparations for war had started in the mid-1930s and in 1935 the Town Council had established an Air Raid Precaution Committee. Recruiting for firefighters and for medical and decontamination units started, and air raid wardens were appointed. Air raid report centres were established in 1938. Here are the wardens of a local reporting post in a private house. Note the strips of sticky paper on the windows, intended to reduce damage from splintering glass caused by bomb blast.

THORNTON HEATH
WINGS FOR VICTORY WEEK
MAY 1st TO 8th
ORGANISED BY
The Thornton Heath (High Street) Traders' Association

A GRAND GALA WEEK
HAS BEEN ARRANGED

Attractions include—

Jack Dowsett & His Happy Rascals

Arthur Sutton's Bright Star & Variety Band
& Company

George Fisher & His Accordian Band

Miss Murchall (late of Jack Paynes Band)

Ivan Withers & His Band

PRESENTED ON

SPECIALLY ERECTED STAGE
(by Messrs. TRUETT & STEEL, LTD.),

AT THE

CORNER OF THE DRIVE,
HIGH STREET, THORNTON HEATH

Also SIDE SHOWS, FIGHTER PLANE,
1,000-lb. BOMB to be dropped on Germany

VALUABLE GIFTS
presented by Local Traders to be Given Away to
HIGHEST BIDDERS.

Highest Bidder gets War Savings to amount Bid, also the Gift.

Roll Up Local Residents and Help Beat Hitler by Buying
WAR SAVING CERTIFICATES

170. To inaugurate Wings for Victory Week in 1943, a mile-long procession marched through the town centre, led by the band of the Royal Canadian Air Force. The town aimed to raise one million pounds in National Savings but actually raised £1,200,755 – the cost of about 240 fighter planes. Thornton Heath traders' efforts contributed £7,217 towards this amount.

171. Croydon, and the Coulsdon and Purley districts, experienced a great deal of bombing. This is an example of the damage caused by a V1 flying bomb ('doodle-bug') which fell in Brigstock Road, Thornton Heath on 16 July 1944. Looking from Quadrant Road, the site of the bomb-damaged houses was laid out after the war as a small park – Trumble Gardens.

172.   During the Second World War over 2,620 high explosive bombs, nine land mines, 141 flying bombs, several V2 rockets and thousands of incendiary bombs fell on Croydon alone with many also on the Urban District of Coulsdon and Purley. In all 747 people were killed, 1,541 seriously injured and 3,000 slightly injured. VJ (Victory over Japan Day), on 15 August 1945, was also the fifth anniversary of the German air raid on Croydon Airport in 1940, and it was widely celebrated. This photograph shows part of the large crowd which gathered in Katharine Street outside the Town Hall at 9.00 pm to hear the King's speech relayed on loud-speakers. At 9.15 p.m. floodlights and a blaze of red, white and blue lamps came on to bathe the Town Hall in light. Large illuminated 'V for Victory' signs were on three sides of the tower, and other buildings were also decorated and illuminated.

Croydon since 1945

The late 1940s were dull days of continuing shortages after the euphoria of Victory. Rationing continued and was even extended; damaged houses and other buildings still needed repair, as maintenance had been neglected and everywhere looked generally run-down. A great housing shortage was alleviated by putting prefabricated houses on to bombed sites and other vacant land. Housing development started again, at first mainly under local council schemes. The small pre-war estate at New Addington was extended and by the 1970s had a population of around 25,000. From the early 1950s private development again gathered pace and later many of the large Victorian houses, by then usually in multi-occupation and at or near the end of 99-year leases, were replaced by flats or smaller houses (e.g. at Park Hill). The remaining agricultural land and small-holdings, such as those at Selsdon, known locally as 'Hungry Bottom' but redeveloped

173. Croydon High Street *c.*1946, looking towards Surrey Street; the no. 42 tram is on its way to Thornton Heath. The Davis Theatre (right) was one of the largest cinema-theatres in the country with some 3,725 seats, and was the venue for concerts, opera, and other stage shows in addition to films. The Royal Philharmonic Orchestra gave its inaugural concert there under Sir Thomas Beecham in 1946, and a visit by the Bolshoi Ballet in 1956 saw queues for tickets reaching to East Croydon station.

The Davis closed and was demolished in 1959 when cinema-going had experienced a serious decline. Several of the shops in this view have most of their windows boarded up, with only small sections of glass – an aftermath of the war.

as Forestdale, were mostly absorbed by redevelopment schemes. Some were converted to school or recreational use, though cattle may still be seen grazing no more than two miles from East Croydon station, and over 3,000 acres of the borough is permanent open space.

In 1951 the remaining local trams were replaced by diesel buses as were the trolley-buses between 1959 and 1960. The airport was closed in 1959 and the last local steam trains ran in the early 1960s.

In 1954 the Borough Development Plan received Ministerial approval and under the Croydon Corporation Act of 1956 the council obtained powers enabling it to redevelop a large part of the town centre. Some 45 acres to the north-east, mainly occupied by schools and large Victorian houses, were set aside for office development. In 1959 the first new office block, Norfolk House, was built and the next 10 years saw a rapid trans-formation of much of the central area. Churches, schools, public houses, theatres and cinemas disappeared to be replaced by roads, car parks, shopping centres and tall office blocks. The Fairfield Halls, opened in 1962, have provided the town with a splendid venue for theatre, music and a wide range of community activities.

The period since 1945 has seen a decline everywhere in local responsibility. Gas and electricity undertakings were nationalised in the late 1940s and when Croydon lost its status as a County Borough in 1965, fire and ambulance services and motor licensing amongst other services passed to other bodies. Water remained under council control but was later transferred to the Thames Water Authority.

There have been numerous other changes. Many immigrants from a wide variety of countries have made Croydon their home and various cultural and racial groups have established themselves in different parts of the northern half of the borough. As church-going has declined so a number of the buildings have either closed (e.g. Laud Street Methodist church, Holy Trinity, Selhurst and St James's) or have been replaced by smaller more appropriate structures (e.g. St Matthew's church formerly in George Street, now at Park Hill). In 1985 Croydon's long association with the Diocese of Canterbury ended when it became part of the Diocese of Southwark, as Coulsdon and Purley were already. Falling rolls and the reorganisation of secondary education has led to the closure of many schools, after a period of much new building in the 1950s. The closures have included some of the large secondary schools such as Selhurst Boys and Girls, Lady Edridge, and even Sylvan (after life as a local education authority school of only 16 years).

The 1980s saw a further spell of new office development and even the demolition and rebuilding of one office block barely 25 years old, with similar developments proposed for the 1990s. Traffic congestion is an ever-increasing problem but environmental schemes in the centre and the pedestrianisation of North End have provided opportunities for street theatre and other entertainment to enliven the main shopping area. In common with most towns some of the local centres have declined in importance and many smaller, family-run shops have been taken over by national chains or closed. Many of the local factories too have closed to be replaced by superstores with large car parks, or warehouses. These superstores and out-of-town retail warehouse developments have in turn led to some reduction of facilities in the main town centre. Grant's department store closed in the early 1980s after over 100 years of trading and a number of shops are now in use as offices or building society branches.

By 1990 nearly 60,000 people worked in the town centre – a far cry from the little market town of barely 150 years earlier.

174. With the serious shortage of housing immediately after the war, Croydon Corporation started a large-scale housing project at New Addington. In this 1956 view, a no. 130 bus on its way out to the growing estate passes a farm tractor in narrow Lodge Lane which at that time was only just wide enough for two vehicles. It was widened a few years later.

175. The first of the new office developments in the town centre was Norfolk House, partly on the site of the old Public Halls. This photograph, taken from the top of a bus in Park Lane on 23 December 1961, shows a Christmas tree on land waiting to be used for road widening and the construction of the underpass. Another new office block is under construction – a very common sight during the 1960s and '70s as cranes and new buildings began to appear in many parts of the town centre.

176. Traffic was removed experimentally from North End in the late 1980s and this arrangement has now been made permanent. Photographed on 21 May 1991, John Whitgift's Hospital of the Holy Trinity, right, is still used for its original purpose as an almshouse, nearly 400 years after it was built. It provides a welcome link with the past, and a contrast with the surrounding buildings of later periods.

177. The site of the Trinity School of John Whitgift and its playing fields between North End and Wellesley Road, was cleared in the 1960s, and offices, car parks and the partially-covered Whitgift Centre with shops on two levels took its place. In the late 1980s a further part of the Whitgift centre was covered and refurbished, as seen here on 3 June 1991.

178. The dramatic transformation of Croydon's skyline is best appreciated from a distance as this aerial photograph taken on 9 May 1991 demonstrates. In the left foreground is Taberner House, the Council offices named after a respected former town clerk, with the Queen's Gardens and the Town Hall tower just visible. In the centre foreground the Fairfield Halls and gardens, and beyond, Croydon College, appear somewhat dwarfed by the tall office blocks flanking Wellesley Road's dual carriageway.

179. The 176 ft. (54 m.) tower of the Town Hall still dominates the townscape in places, as seen from North End on Monday 3 June 1991. The Drummond Centre and Debenham's are on the right and Allders is on the left. For the first time in centuries people now have precedence over vehicles here and can, if they wish, sit and relax during shopping expeditions, and, from time to time, enjoy music and other entertainment. This is perhaps an encouraging sign for the future of an ancient town which has been a trading centre for more than 700 years.

High Street looking south in 1830.